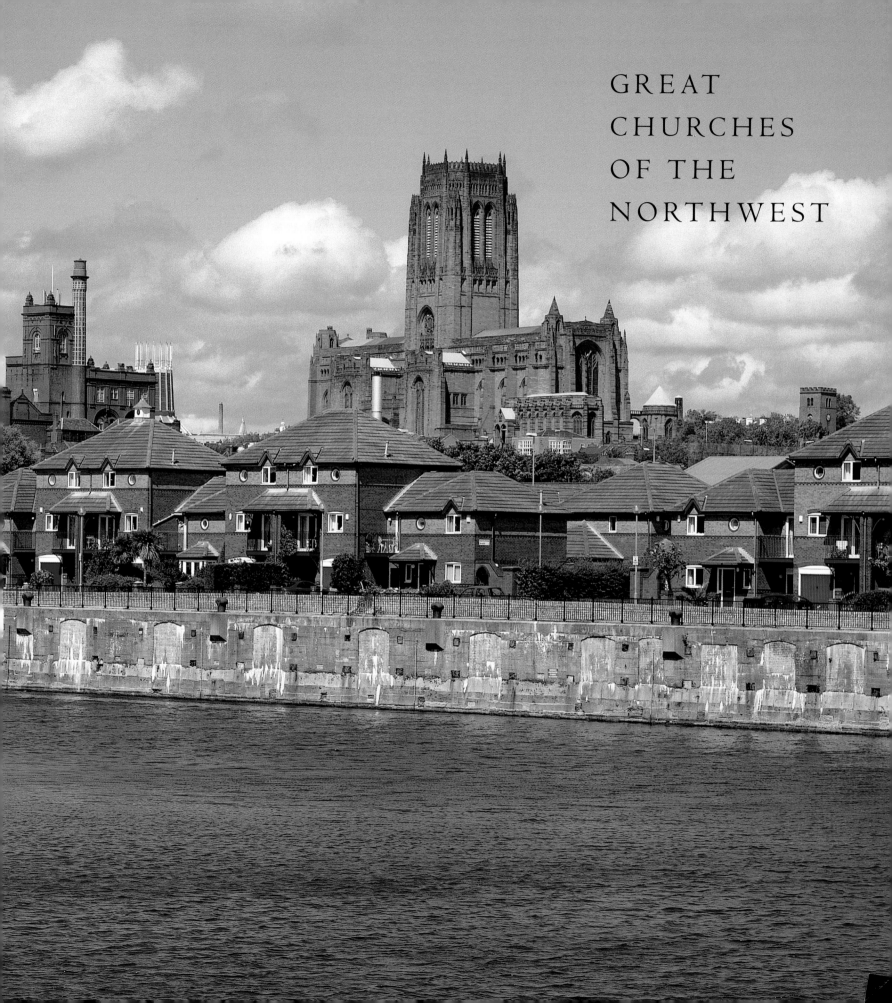

GREAT
CHURCHES
OF THE
NORTHWEST

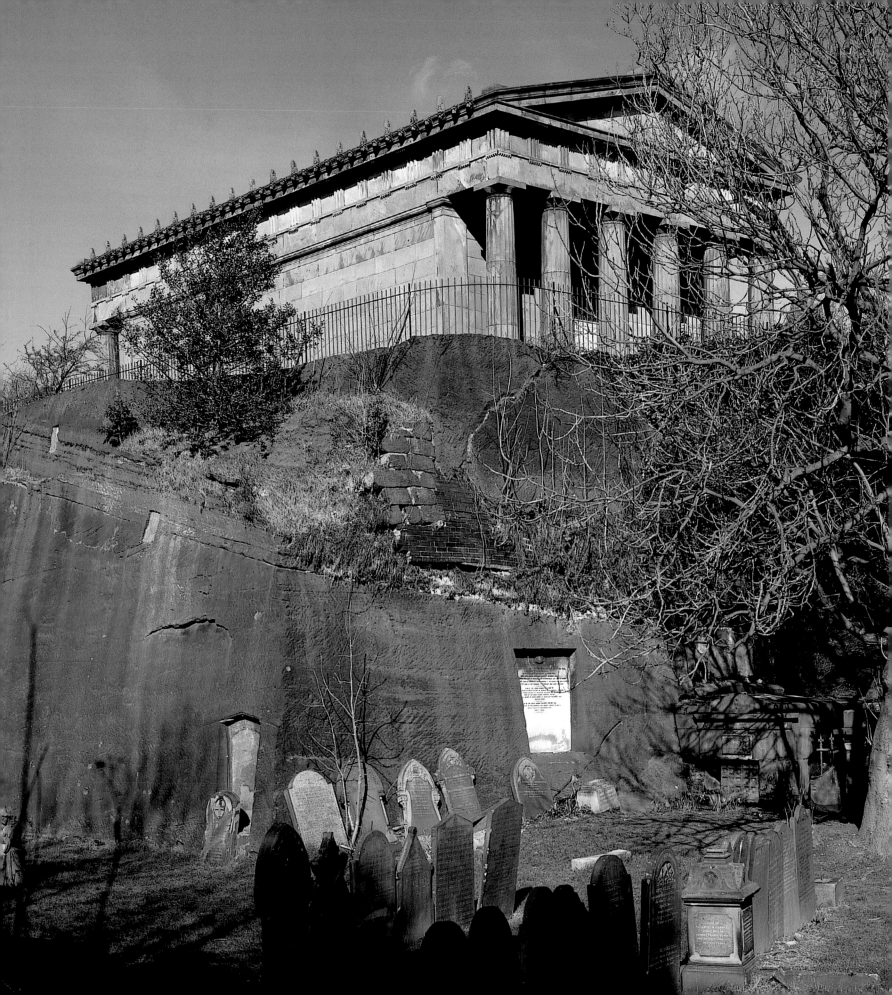

GREAT CHURCHES OF THE NORTHWEST

Matthew Byrne

FRANCES LINCOLN LIMITED

PUBLISHERS

Frances Lincoln Ltd, 4 Torriano Mews,
Torriano Avenue, London NW5 2RZ
www.franceslincoln.com

Great Churches of the Northwest
Copyright © Frances Lincoln Ltd 2008
Text and photographs © Matthew Byrne 2008

First Frances Lincoln edition 2008

A catalogue record for this book is available from the British Library.

ISBN: 978-0-7112-2916-7

Printed and bound in Singapore.

9 8 7 6 5 4 3 2 1

HALF TITLE Liverpool Cathedral seen from the Brunswick
dock alongside the River Mersey.

TITLE PAGE The Oratory, the cemetery chapel at Liverpool
Cathedral.

THIS PAGE St Michael Hawkshead, with panoramic views
of the mountains beyond.

CONTENTS

PREFACE

For the purpose of these photographic portraits of selected churches, the northwest of England is taken to comprise Cumbria, Lancashire, Greater Manchester and Merseyside. Before the county boundaries reorganisation of 1974 Cumbria existed as Cumberland and Westmorland and Lancashire included Greater Manchester and Merseyside.

The area of the region is large, too large it might be thought for a book such as this to provide a representative selection of all its churches. However, as far as interesting churches are concerned (the criteria for that description is given below) the northwest is not in the same league as say Norfolk, Suffolk, Lincolnshire, Devon and other counties. In the Middle Ages the region was one of the most sparsely populated in England with correspondingly few churches. Even now there are some areas of more than 100 square miles where there are few if any churches, among them the Scottish borders, the Lake District and the Forest of Bowland in Lancashire. Before the Reformation the average area of a parish in Norfolk was three square miles and in the south of England generally it averaged five square miles. In Cumbria it was twenty-four square miles and in Lancashire thirty-five. As individual examples in the latter two the parish of Kendal (Cumbria) was 100 square miles while Whalley parish (Lancashire), which took in the Forest of Bowland, was a remarkable 170 square miles. After the Reformation the seventeenth century added a mere handful of churches and the eighteenth century only a relatively modest number. The massive increase in the population of the region's cities and towns in the nineteenth and twentieth centuries following the Industrial Revolution led to the widespread division of parishes and to the building of thousands of new churches in the Victorian and later periods. But while these often remain the much-loved centres of worshipping communities (and that is what a church is for), the vast majority of these newcomers has no claim to architectural distinction or to the interest of architectural historians or the ordinary church explorers for

whom this book is intended. As a result the task of making an adequately representative selection of interesting churches has not been as difficult as it might appear.

The selection has been made on the basis of a number of criteria:

- Architectural distinction as understood by architectural historians and critics.
- Picturesque quality, either externally or internally as recognised and enjoyed by the typical church lover. In this category are included several small, humble churches that have no claim at all under the first criterion. These are often churches which have retained their original medieval or eighteenth-century fittings and furnishings to give that 'atmospheric' feeling that visitors instantly recognise. The ruthless restorations of the Victorian period stripped many churches of their ancient stonework without and their equally ancient furnishings within, thus making them indistinguishable from new churches of the time.
- Outstanding quality of sculpture, monuments, woodwork, metalwork, stained glass, etc.
- An association with an interesting person such as rector, patron or parishioner who founded or contributed to the church in some way.
- Attractiveness of setting whether in country or town.

All of the churches selected for this volume satisfy two or more of these criteria but so also do a considerable number of others not included. The final choice has been personal: the churches photographed and described here have given me great pleasure on the many occasions that I have visited them. Some readers will inevitably be surprised by the exclusions of their own favourites. Whatever the limitations of the present selection it cannot be said that it lacks variety or comprehensiveness. The period covered by these portraits ranges from the seventh century to the late twentieth century. The churches are situated in the remotest countryside, in villages, towns, suburbs and city centres. They embrace every architectural style, Saxon, Norman, Gothic, classical and modern. They include buildings that are large enough to seat 2,000 people and those that would be crowded with a congregation of 100.

One recent writer on churches believes that in modern times they are mainly museums of art and local history (and a book of this kind can sometimes implicitly contribute to that view). For some visiting them that may be so but it is clearly not the view of the several million people in this country who use them for regular worship. Viewed only as works of art and reminders of history churches can give considerable pleasure, but for those who share the beliefs and the aspirations of the people who built them, or have some empathy with those beliefs, a purely artistic appreciation can deepen into affection and love. The late John Betjeman's self-confessed 'passion for churches' is an illustration of that. Lover of English architecture and landscape, poet laureate (1972–84), essayist, broadcaster and scourge of all those who would destroy beautiful things from the past for commercial gain, he wrote movingly – and entertainingly – of that passion. It is vividly conveyed in the Introduction to his *Guide to English Parish Churches* which combines his knowledge of architecture, art and church history with a religious faith and with his affectionate understanding of the work, beliefs, virtues and foibles of countless generations of clergy and laity who have built, cared for and continuously beautified the churches of England right up to the present day.

The best way to explore a church is by a personal visit but for those who are unable to make the journeys, which are quite extensive in this case, or who wish to revive happy memories it is hoped that these photographs and the text that supports them will give some pleasure.

Matthew Byrne, 2008

Bewcastle

Lanercost

Brampton

Brougham

Martindale

CUMBRIA

Hawkshead

Cartmel Fell

Cartmel

Kirkby Lonsdale

Lancaster

Pilling

Slaidburn

Great Mitton

Whalley

LANCASHIRE

Leyland

Standish

Middleton

Sefton

Salford

MANCHESTER

LIVERPOOL

INTRODUCTION

Factors that affect the external character of a church or any other building include its situation, its age and hence its likely architectural style and the materials of which it is built.

The situation and surroundings of a church are capable of creating impressions and lasting memories even if the architecture is relatively undistinguished. The little seventeenth-century church of St Ninian at Brougham, Cumbria (pages 28–33) is interesting in its own right but what makes it so enduringly memorable is its isolation among the fells about a mile from the nearest road. From some of the small rustic churches of the Lake District there are stunning panoramic views of the mountains (pages 34–6). Not surprisingly in northwest England dramatic hilltop sites are quite common in both cities and countryside. From a Lancaster priory churchyard on top of a steep hill the view to the east is over the town and to the west over Morecambe Bay and the Cumbrian hills twenty miles beyond (pages 44–7). In Middleton, Greater Manchester, its late medieval church is perched on top of a town hill overlooking a landscape dotted with nineteenth-century mills and factories that L.S. Lowry might have painted (pages 72–7). The little church of Great Mitton, Lancashire, and the cluster of houses around it on top of a small hill dropping down to the River Ribble are somewhat reminiscent of a hill village in one of the Mediterranean countries (pages 55–8). High on a ridge overlooking the River Mersey the greatest of all the churches in this book, the Anglican Cathedral Church of Christ towers over the city and the docks (pages 98–104). Nowhere are there churches with surroundings more varied than in the northwest either in the form of natural landscapes or man-made townscapes. It gives, I hope, a special appeal to the photographs.

On the bases of geography and population northwest England divides into two clear-cut areas, a northern half made up of Cumbria and Lancashire and a southern half comprising Merseyside in the southwest and Greater Manchester in the southeast, although there is a curious hybrid, transitional area between them. The contrast in the scenery that surrounds their churches could hardly be greater.

The northern half is not only overwhelmingly rural, it has some of the loneliest and wildest landscapes in England. The northernmost part of the former Cumberland that runs down from the Scottish border is an open landscape of low, rolling hills where the traveller on foot or in a car has panoramic views for miles around in all directions. A little further south is the Lake District National Park where the hills are higher and closer together forming the steep-sided valleys and the lakes themselves. This is the most dramatic scenery in England and one of its favourite places for walkers and climbers. South again and we are in Lancashire where the lakes disappear but the hills and the moors continue until we reach the vast Forest of Bowland which covers much of the rest of the county. This is a place of low hills, bare on the tops but well wooded below where there are innumerable fast-flowing rivers and streams. Sparsely populated with no towns and few villages, it is a walkers' paradise, a far cry from the Lancashire of popular imagination which always pictured the county as formerly defined solely in terms of its grimy industrial south, such as the cities of Liverpool, Salford and Manchester. In fact, with the latter now separated from it, Lancashire is predominately a rural county. It is true to say that visitors to the whole of this northern half of the region we are considering go there for the scenery rather than the architecture (a situation that might be reversed in, say, inland Norfolk). But throughout Cumbria and Lancashire there are many churches large and small to be viewed against the magnificent background of mountains, moors and lakes.

Leaving Lancashire we leave the the northern rural half of the region but we do not pass directly into the urban south. A line that runs eastwards from Preston on the coast to the Pennines passes near the former mill towns of Blackburn, Bolton and Bury, and the land on either side of it forms that hybrid region referred to above. The landscape is still predominantly one of hills and moors cut by steep narrow valleys with the rivers at their bottoms that provided the power for the first phase of the Industrial Revolution here. The towns are compactly sited in the valleys so that even in their centres one can often see the rather bleak, forbidding moors above. Conversely, hikers on the moors who at one moment are contemplating nothing more than coarse grass and heather can round the side of a hill to find themselves looking down on tall mill chimneys surrounded by a network of streets lined with terraced houses. It was this that was in the mind of William Blake when he referred to 'our clouded hills' and 'dark satanic mills' in 'England's green and pleasant lands' (pages 72–7).

Just a few miles further south we enter the unmistakable southern half of the region covered by this book, Merseyside to the west and Greater Manchester to the east. This is one of the largest industrial connurbations in the world, housing a population to match it. It includes the cities of Liverpool, Salford and Manchester, and many large towns such as Warrington, Widnes, St Helens, Wigan, Oldham and many more. In fact a traveller may well pass from one to another without being conscious of any separation as the outer parts of one often merge into the outer parts of the next where tarmacadam, concrete and brick reign supreme. Many of the older industries on which the prosperity of the area was first based have all but disappeared, coal and cotton among them, while the older chemical industries such as the chlor-alkali industry based on Cheshire salt, and soap and brick manufacture have been joined by petro-chemicals, plastics, electronics and motor manufacturing.

Sufficient has been said about the landscapes surrounding the churches of the northwest and we now turn to a brief summary of the architectural history of the churches themselves. Although there is fragmentary evidence of churches or at least places of worship in England before the Saxon period and the arrival of St Augustine and his companion monk-missionaries in Kent in AD 597, the earliest Christian architecture dates from about this time, continuing until the Norman Conquest in 1066. There are about 500 surviving churches in England that are wholly or partly of this period but they are little represented in the northwest. The little ruined chapel at Heysham on the Lancashire coast built about AD 800 now hardly counts as architecture nor do the traces of Saxon work that have survived in other places.

The late Norman west dorway (c.1170) at St Mary, Kirkby Lonsdale, typically Romanesque in its ornately carved round-headed arches.

complete Norman church has something of the atmosphere of a contemporary castle, powerful, earthy and majestically austere. There are now no churches in the region that are entirely Norman (eight hundred years of constant alterations and extensions have seen to that). Apart from Carlisle Cathedral, the most impressive monument to the period is the nave of Kirkby Lonsdale church, Cumbria (pages 42–3) which exemplifies all the characteristics of Norman architecture mentioned above. The Normans frequently expended considerable effort and skill in the decoration of chancel arches, doorways and fonts and these can be found in several parish churches (pages 37–41, 72–7). It is evidence of the phenomenal physical energy, spiritual convictions and the material ambitions of a race of people who had arrived in England only in 1066 that they had within a generation penetrated to the northern limits of William the Conqueror's new kingdom.

The most important piece of Saxon work in the northwest – and it is of the first importance nationally and internationally – is not a church at all but a cross, the Bewcastle cross near the Scottish border (pages 16–19). Dated to the late seventh century it is carved overall with a variety of subjects, work that has been described as the finest of its kind in Europe at that time. There are a number of Viking crosses in the region, a legacy of the Viking invasions when armies from Denmark and Norway landed on the Cumbrian and Lancashire coasts in the ninth and tenth centuries (pages 59–65).

The Romanesque style of architecture of the period c.1080–1200, known as Norman in England, is much better represented in towns and villages. It is the style of the round-headed arch of ancient Rome (which gives the style its name) and also of massively thick walls with small windows. Naves are separated from aisles by piers of elephantine proportions with a wide variety of characteristic capitals. The often prolific decoration of all parts of the buildings takes the form of mouldings with the ubiquitous zig-zag and other geometric forms, together with some figure carving, commonly in the form of grotesque animal and human heads. A

Norman architecture gave way to the very different Gothic style in c.1200. It is the architecture of the pointed arch (although this has more significance than mere shape), rib-vaulted stone roofs, flying buttresses and large windows whose heads are filled with intricate stone tracery. The Gothic style came to England from France just as Norman Romanesque had done but thereafter developed, at least partly, in its own characteristic way, passing through three developing phases. The first was Early English Gothic, c.1200–50, readily recognised as you approach a church by its tall, narrow lancet windows arranged either singly or in stepped groupings. Decoration is restrained and the atmosphere inside is one of quiet calm. It is not widely represented in our region, the best examples being in those parish churches that were formerly monastic, e.g. Lanercost (pages 20–3) and Cartmel (pages 37–41). The second period was Decorated Gothic, c.1250–1350. As the name suggests this is characterised by more sculptural decoration than its predecessor, most notably perhaps in the treatment of windows whose upper parts now have stone tracery formed either from relatively simple geometrical patterns based on the circle and its quadrants (the earlier Geometric Decorated) or on much more complicated sinuous forms (the later Flowing or Curvilinear Decorated). The mouldings on piers, arches and around windows were also more complex and there was an abundance on walls, doorways and capitals of carvings of charming little heads, human, animal and grotesque, which all adds up to a spirit of great liveliness. Again it is little represented in the northwest and then only in the larger churches. The third, Perpendicular, phase lasted the longest of all, from 1350 up to the Reformation in the mid-sixteenth century and even, in so far as church building continued immediately after that, right into the early seventeenth century. The style derives its name from the fact that the mullions in the windows now continued vertically upwards through the tracery to the arch above, windows which were now even larger than formerly producing walls that were more glass than stone. This produced interiors of great light and clarity, enhanced by slender piers separating naves from aisles and more

Early sixteenth-century choir stalls at St Helen, Sefton. The bench ends have carved decoration and poppy heads.

in that they were sensitive and sympathetic to the original character of the building. Most were not, often involving virtual rebuilding externally and internally. It is fair to say as a measure of defence that the eighteenth century had neglected these churches dreadfully. Religious apathy (or at least an absence of enthusiasm) combined with a widespread contempt of the medieval Gothic style when classical architecture was favoured by the intellectual classes was the cause of this apathy. However, the Victorians went to the opposite extreme. The Gothic style had returned to favour but most of the leaders of opinion in architecture favoured the 'Middle Pointed' (i.e. Decorated) Gothic. The Early English was regarded as 'immature' and the later Perpendicular as 'debased'. As a result their restorations involved sweeping away those parts of a church in the unfavoured styles and replacing them with the favoured period. Inside these churches old furnishings, some of them of great historical importance and artistic quality

unified interiors. Many churches that started life as Norman, Early English or Decorated buildings were transformed into this latest style as clergy and parishioners looked for larger and brighter churches and, no doubt, sought to be as up-to-date as possible. Three excellent examples of this transformation are at Standish (pages 69–71) and Middleton (pages 72–7), both Greater Manchester, and Sefton, Merseyside (pages 94–7).

It is in Cumbria and Lancashire that all these medieval churches, Norman and Gothic, best retain their original character. The larger ones include those that were once monastic, Cartmel and Lanercost already mentioned and Lancaster (pages 44–7). The smaller ones, built for equally small isolated communities populating the fells are characteristically low and rugged as though clinging to the hillsides for protection against the harshness of the weather. Cartmel Fell (page 36) and Brougham (pages 28–33), both in Cumbria are typical of them. These northernmost churches retain their medieval character because they were left almost untouched by the Victorians. In England as a whole over 7,000 medieval churches out of a total of 9,000 were 'restored' in the reign of Queen Victoria. Some of these were restrained

were thrown out wholesale. High Churchmen particularly disliked eighteenth-century box pews and three-decker pulpits, while Low Churchmen disliked rood screens and eleborate altars. All of this was more likely to happen in the cities and towns where the necessary finance was available. In Merseyside and Greater Manchester no more than a dozen medieval churches survive in anything like their original state. The churches at Middleton and Sefton (above) are two of the best.

In Italy in the early fifteenth century, architects in Florence and Rome rejected Gothic for a return to the classical architecture of ancient Rome the ruins of which were all around them. The English, not having this inspiration and being inherently more conservative were at the time untouched by this. A century later, when such ideas might have begun to diffuse across the English Channel, Henry VIII in his break with the Pope and with Rome had effectively isolated the country from continental influences for some time to come. It was not until the mid-seventeenth century that classical architecture was used in churches to a significant extent, later than in domestic architecture. In any event there was a negligible amount of church building for a hundred years after the Henrician reformation. Having said this, there is a remarkably early example even by London standards, of a transition from Gothic to classical in Standish church in a rebuilding of 1582–4 (pages 69–71).

The rare examples of church building in the provinces in the seventeenth century are usually due to the influence – and affluence – of determined and single-minded individuals, that at Brougham, Cumbria (pages 28–33) being an excellent example.

By the beginning of the eighteenth century the classical style of architecture was dominant in England, Gothic rejected. There are many fine churches of the period in all parts of the northwest. Georgian architects had an unrivalled ability to produce the most elegant and harmonious buildings from the simplest plans and elevations. Roman or Greek temples were used as the basic model for churches. The plans were usually simple rectangles with nave and chancel in one. At the western end the entrance might be

The two-decker pulpit, with the royal arms of George I dated 1719 on the wall behind, at Pilling church, Lancashire.

with large mansions for the very wealthy and rows of large elegant terraced houses lining streets where the only noises then were the clatter of horses' hooves and the clatter of the carriages they pulled. An impressive new classical church would be part of this new developement at a time when church going and respectability were closely linked. As the cities and towns expanded in the nineteenth and twentieth centuries the wealthy were pushed ever further out. The mansions and large terraced houses are now in the twenty-first century sub-divided into flats, often ill-maintained. The large gardens have suffered infill development with cheap modern housing. So the elegant churches often stand today in surroundings very different from those in which they were built. St Philip's, Salford (pages 91–3) is a good example. (In fairness to local councils in Liverpool, Manchester, Salford and elsewhere it should be said that the last twenty years have seen an enormous improvement visually and socially in such areas.)

a giant columned portico rising to the full height of the building, or if finance was limited a much simpler doorway with a small pediment above. Windows along the sides of the nave are relatively large and, of course round-headed, clear glass being favoured. Interiors were filled with box pews with doors to the aisle and seating around three or four sides. The east ends of the chancels have handsome altar reredoses often carved by craftsmen with the highest skills. Chancels are separated from naves by communion rails with finely turned balusters. To the left or right of this a giant three-decker pulpit would dominate much of the interior. From the latter Georgian clergy, wigged and gowned, would preach at often inordinate length. Classical churches were built in every kind of parish. Landed aristocrats and gentry built them on their estates (convenient for the big house). In market towns churchwardens sometimes preferred to demolish dilapidated medieval churches rather than repair them. In the industrial cities and in the mill towns of the region the wealthy factory owners and the merchants wanted to move their residences away from the factories and the surrounding slums which had produced their wealth. New residential areas were created at the edges of cities and towns

In the nineteenth century the Victorians were no less enthusiastic about building new churches than they were in restoring old ones (above). In Victoria's reign about 6,000 new churches were built on new sites, i.e. approximately 100 for each year of her reign. Not only was the population of the country as a whole increasing, there was a marked shift from country to town. The northwest had its fair share of this new building. The architectural tables were now turned once again. Classical architecture for churches (and many other buildings) was rejected; only the Gothic style was now considered suitable. Among the leaders of opinion in this regard were Augustus W.N. Pugin, John Ruskin and others. The change was not simply on aesthetic or artistic grounds. Pugin in particular regarded it as an abomination that a Christian church should be built in the form of a pagan Greek or Roman temple. For Pugin the Middle Ages were the golden age of Christianity in England and Europe. The Middle Ages used Gothic architecture; therefore, he argued with considerable passion, Gothic was the only style for a Christian church. Zealous incumbents or their patrons were the spearhead of the building campaign. The Anglo-Catholic and Evangelical wings of the Church of England were particularly involved in a significant religious revival to capture the working classes for Christ. If the rector, patron of the living or the parishioners were wealthy, the most distinguished architects of the day could be employed with truly spectacular results that could vie with anything that the Middle Ages could produce. These new 'Gothic Revival' churches were not necessarily a slavish copy of medieval Gothic. The style was adapted to suit the situation, the views of the patron and his rector on liturgical matters – and of course the money available. In the years 1850–80 many architects favoured bold, almost aggressive forms of the style with heavy massing of the parts that could be seen at a distance such as towers and spires. Detailing such as pinnacles, finials, buttresses, window tracery and the capitals of piers inside had a similiar boldness which could not be mistaken for their medieval counterparts. Architects liked to use several materials to give

Nineteenth-century Catholic art frequently aimed for the emotional jugular. This example, showing Christ scourged before His crucifixion, is at Holy Name of Jesus, Manchester.

polychromatic effects. Interiors too were lavishly embellished with ornate coloured designs painted or stencilled on walls and ceilings and the ubiquitous encaustic tiles for floors. In the later Victorian period leading architects such as G.F. Bodley (pages 105–9) and J.L. Pearson (pages 110–15) turned to gentler, more refined forms of the style, closer to the medieval.

Work of the first half of the twentieth century was largely an uninspired continuation of the Gothic Revival without either the conviction or the finance of the earlier period. The last forty years of the century saw architects producing innovative designs, often with 'central' plans to conform with modern liturgical thinking which demanded that congregations be more closely linked with the officiating priest. The pre-eminent example of this in the region is the Roman Catholic cathedral in Liverpool by Frederick Gibberd, built 1962–7 (pages 116–23). A good example of a parish church is St Mary, Leyland, Lancashire (pages 66–8).

It has been said that situation, architectural style and its building materials create the character of a church and having briefly outlined how the first two of these are seen in northwest churches we turn now to the third. The choice of material to build a church usually depends on the resources of the region (unless, as is only rarely the case one is prepared to import materials entirely from outside) and as a result buildings have a distinct regional character and the northwest is no exception. In view of the size of the area it is not surprising that there are equally distinct sub-regional variations.

Traditionally the preferred material for prestigious buildings intended to endure has been stone. This prefernce long pre-dates the Middle Ages in England, going back to ancient Greece and Rome. Other factors being equal architects and patrons will prefer to use local stone if only for reasons of economy. Exceptions today generally involve wealthy organisations erecting headquarters buildings or offices in modern city centres who in order to make them stand out and impress use 'flashier' stones, often from abroad. Sir Frederick Gibberd, although not working for a wealthy client chose Portland stone from the Dorset coast for his Roman Catholic cathedral in Liverpool. Its pure brilliant whiteness makes for a startling contrast with the surrounding buildings and the stone has established a reputation for standing up remarkably well to the polluted atmospheres of English cities – witness its use by Sir Christopher Wren in the seventeenth century for the rebuilding of St Paul's cathedral and the churches of the City of London. However, all other churches described here have been built with a regional stone.

Good building stones are in abundant supply in northwest England and that reveals itself in the churches of the region because what is seen above the ground depends on what is below the ground. The dominant stones here by far are the sandstones. Grains of sand as seen on any beach are composed of a crystalline form of silica known as quartz, an oxide of the element silicon (to chemists SiO_2). Quartz is one of the physically hardest and chemically most resistant materials in existence. It is used in chemical manufacturing plants to resist attack by the most corrosive materials at very high temperatures. Sandstone is formed when sand grains become cemented together over a long period of time under the pressure of materials above. The cementation of the grains into stone occurs as water containing dissolved substances seeps through the sand and then dries out, leaving the former dissolved substances as a cement. The way in which the sandstone so formed reacts to time and weathering in a building depends not on the hard, durable grains of sand but on the nature of the cementing material which varies with the nature of the environment within which the Sandstone was formed. The widely contrasting character of different sandstones is strikingly demonstrated in those of northwest England. Quartz itself is pure white as seen on some western beaches of Scotland and Ireland. Elsewhere it is always coloured by the presence of traces of iron oxides. There are several of these depending on the degree of oxidation of the iron. There are two colour groups; one from the palest buff through to golden yellow; the second from the palest

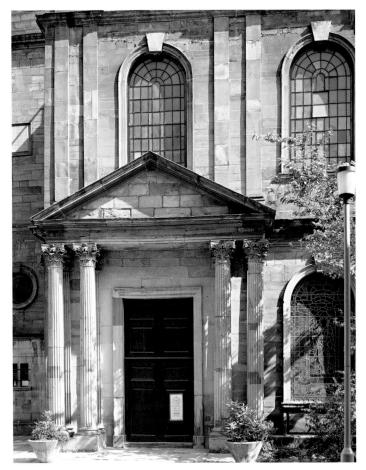

St Anne's church, Manchester, is built of several differently coloured northern sandstones.

Since the Carboniferous period covers a considerable time-span the sandstones within vary considerably in age. One of the most common is Millstone Grit sandstone. (It was actually used in making millstones because of its hardness.) The colours of carboniferous sandstones belong to the buff-golden group, the buff sometimes rather greyish and subdued, the golden sometimes gloriously warm almost like a Cotswold limestone.

The other, equally important sandstone in the northwest is one laid down in the Triassic period, 190–225 million years ago, rather younger than the Carboniferous. It is often called New Red Sandstone because the colours often belong to the second, pink to deep red colour group described above. Confusingly, the colours are by no means always red, buff being quite common. It is the sandstone of much of the western coastal areas from Cumbria down through Lancashire and Merseyside where it spreads eastwards to occupy the

pink through to deep red. These are therefore the colours we see in the region's churches. In fact until recently the natural colour of stonework in an old building in the northwest was irrelevant. The gritty surfaces of sandstones adhere tenaciously to the solid particles in the grime-laden atmospheres of the northwest, polluted by centuries of chimney smoke from a million houses, factories and mills. The Clean Air Acts of the late twentieth century followed by widespread stone cleaning operations have dramatically changed some of the most dreary and dismal townscapes in England into a variety of more colourful and handsome façades.

The oldest sandstone in our region was formed in the geological period known as the Carboniferous, 280–350 million years ago, at the same time as the region's abundant supply of coal was formed, the fact that gives the period its name. It is the stone of the Pennines and hence in our case the regions adjoining them, East Lancashire and parts of Greater Manchester. The cementing material is here itself silicaceous so that the resulting stone is as hard and durable as any. This did not make it easy for the masons to cut in former times but it does make it an enduringly weather-resistant stone.

southern parts of Greater Manchester. From here it continues downwards into Cheshire and the Welsh border counties. Apart from its colour it is in marked contrast as a building stone to the Carboniferous sandstones. The material cementing the sand grains is quite weak, clay-like and calcareous, and these stones are among the least durable in England. The cathedrals and churches of this part of the region have suffered badly from weathering. Wind, rain and particularly the acidic constituents of polluted atmospheres have caused it to disintegrate badly. Churches here have had to endure constant stone replacement work as a result. (The great Anglican cathedral in Liverpool built of this sandstone from a quarry in the southeast of the city is still too recent to have proved itself, pages 98–104). To summarise, therefore, the sandstone churches portrayed in the book fall into a west–east divide, those in the west of the red, younger stone and those in the east of the older buff stones. However, to see what is a veritable geological museum of regional sandstones one must walk around the outside of St Ann's church in Manchester city centre (pages 82–5) where there are no less than five differently coloured sandstones, a remarkable and unique mixture.

Limestone appears in parts of Cumbria including the Lake District. Chemically limestone is calcium carbonate (to chemists, $CaCO_3$) and like the sandstones limestones were laid down in several different geological periods. The limestone in Cumbria is a silver-grey Carboniferous stone, similar to that seen in the Yorkshire Dales. It appears in the churches at Cartmel (pages 37–41) and Kirkby Lonsdale (pages 42–3).

Slate occurs and is widely used in Cumbria as a building wall-stone (e.g. at Martindale church, pages 34–5) as well, of course as a universally popular roofing material. Slate is a hard, weather-resistant silicate, usually mid- to dark-blue although some of the Lakeland quarries yield a distinctive and attractive green stone.

Brick is sometimes regarded as a lowly substitute for stone but this is not necessarily true at all. In the eighteenth century when the use of brick became widespread the Georgians created the most attractive churches (and of course houses) in brick, a material now mellowed to any number of warm, attractive shades. Stone dressings, however, do enhance the attractiveness. When entirely hand-made before the nineteenth-century brick could be an expensive material, as much so as stone in some areas, but that changed with the mechanisation of the industry when factories could turn out bricks by the million each week. Machine-made brick generally has a much harder, glossier surface than the earlier hand-made varieties. The clays of the northwest lend themselves well to brickmaking. The bricks of Accrington, Lancashire, are famous in the region, the clay and the manufacturing conditions producing a very bright red, hard glazed brick. Some of the most famous Victorian churches in the northwest are constructed of bricks like this, including J.L. Pearson's famous church of St Agnes, Liverpool (pages 110–15), although the interior, remarkably, is of stone. People seem to love or loathe this particular brick in equal numbers.

In the last thirty years architects of distinction have used materials such as concrete, glass, metal and others in various innovative designs for churches (pages 66–8, 116–23).

It is rewarding to observe closely and to try and identify the building materials of a church and how they have withstood the passage of time; it adds greatly to the enjoyment of a visit.

Note

The churches and works of art described in this book span thirteen hundred years but there seemed no particular advantage in arranging the churches chronologically, nor arranging them alphabetically by place name. Instead the chosen churches have been described geographically from the Scottish border in the north to the River Mersey in the south. If read consecutively this may provide a sense of a journey down through the region. The chapters are, however, self-contained and may be read in any order.

Sources of information

The principal sources of historical and other information used in the text are listed in the 'Bibliography and Acknowledgements'. Some sources have been used too frequently to acknowledge at every point in the text but when the opinion of a named authority on a piece of architecture or art has been quoted verbatim in the text the source of the quotation will be found in this section.

Access

Churches vary greatly in the degree of access that can be given to visitors outside of services. One church in this book is never locked, day or night but because of the danger of theft (and more frequently these days, mindless vandalism) some churches have to be continuously locked between services. Cathedrals and larger historic churches are usually open and staffed each day. Others are open on a limited basis. In order to help readers who may wish to see the interiors of churches photographed here I have given an indication of the access available. This should be taken only as a general guide based on my personal experience. Visitors travelling any distance should make appropriate enquiries beforehand.

THE BEWCASTLE CROSS, CUMBRIA

OUTSTANDING SAXON SCULPTURE ON A REMOTE NORTHERN FRONTIER

The south face of the Bewcastle Cross: separate panels of knot-work and vine scrolls.

With the exception of the little ruined chapel at Heysham on the Lancashire coast, which now no longer counts as architecture, there is no church in this northwest region of England that is wholly or mainly of the Anglo-Saxon period. But since Saxon Christianity spanned such a long period of English history from around AD 600 to the Norman Conquest in 1066 and made so many contributions to that history, the lack of any reference to it would leave a significant gap in a book like this. Fortunately the gap can be filled because just south of the Scottish border there is a smaller but nonetheless outstanding monument of the early English Christian church in the form of a splendidly carved stone cross. By coincidence, therefore, the start of our journey based on geography is also the start of our story based on history.

Bewcastle is a widely and thinly scattered settlement of farms and cottages seven miles south of the Scottish border and now an exceptionally remote place. Visitors from the south will approach it by a series of diminishing roads: first a motorway, then A roads, B roads, and finally narrow unfenced by-roads. The last stage of the journey is an exhilarating one. The western end of border country is a land of low, round-topped hills widely spaced so that there are panoramic views for miles in all directions. At one point near Bewcastle one can look back southwards for a distance of about thirty miles to the mountains of the Lake District and northwards into Scotland for about fifteen miles. The area contains the Kielder National Park and several forests. By the sides of the roads there are indicators of past life on a border plagued in the past by warfare and pillage. A number of pele towers can be seen, small tower-houses that had animal shelters on the ground floor and quarters for family on the first floor, which when necessary could be accessed only by ladder.

The purpose of our journey to Bewcastle is to see the work of a community of Christian Saxons, but these were not the first important visitors to reach it. Bewcastle is about six miles north of Hadrian's Wall, the great Roman defensive work built from the second century AD onwards to defend conquered England from the unconquered peoples further north. At Bewcastle, on the site of a pagan Celtic shrine, the Romans built an outpost fort on the 'barbarian' side of the wall from which troops could monitor and report on any suspicious

The west face of the Bewcastle cross. From top to bottom: St John the Baptist holding a Lamb of God; Christ with a scroll in His left hand raises the other in blessing; Saxon runes dating the cross; St John the Evangelist holding an eagle. The wide open landscape of the border country can be seen in the background.

The east face: a continuous vine scroll inhabited by beasts and birds shows considerable artistic sophistication.

movements of potential invaders heading south. Parts of the earthwork defences are still visible on a natural plateau above a little beck enclosing a hexagonal area of approximately six acres. At the height of its occupation the fort was manned by 800 men. Although it was a military site, archaeological finds have indicated a community of considerable culture and artistic taste. Finds include a silver plaque of a warrior god and, even more remarkably, pieces of verde antico, a green marble from the Peloponesian islands of Greece. But yet more remarkable art was later to find its way to Bewcastle.

Some time after the Romans withdrew from Britain in AD 411 their fort at Bewcastle became the home for a group of Anglo-Saxons who then had no knowledge of Christianity. The cross at Bewcastle was the creation of their distant Christian descendants. The cross, the churchyard in which it stands and the small, much later medieval church were all built within the Roman fort. The cross has lost its head, leaving its stone shaft standing about fourteen feet above a plinth. Each of the four faces is entirely covered with carvings. An inscription in runes (the script of the earliest Germanic alphabet used by Scandinavians and Anglo-Saxons) on the west face refers to King Alcfrith of Saxon Northumbria, son of King Oswin who was killed in a battle in AD 676. This apparently dates the cross to about the same time, although because of considerable weathering and erosion of the runes some scholars dispute the reading. A date of about this time is however accepted by many. The cross is unique in its variety; there is sacred figure sculpture, animal and foliage sculpture and the complex abstract knot-interlace work so familiar from contemporary Celtic and Saxon art. It is also unique in the quality of the work, which Pevsner describes as 'amazingly high . . . there is nothing as perfect of a comparable date in Europe'. The west face of the cross has at the top the figure

The original Norman castle beside the church was built to defend the border lands between England and Scotland. It was rebuilt in this form in the fourteenth century within the earthworks of a Roman fort, showing how many different peoples have come to this remote spot in the past.

of St John the Baptist holding an Agnus Dei (Lamb of God). Below this is a figure of Christ, his right hand raised in blessing and carrying a scroll in the other. His feet stand on the heads of two animals. Then there is the runic inscription referred to above. At the bottom is a figure interpreted as St John the Evangelist holding an eagle, his traditional symbol. The south face is carved entirely with separate panels of abstract designs, knot-work and vine scrolls. The east face, on the other hand, is carved with one continuous scheme: a vine scroll inhabited by beasts and birds. The way in which these face alternate ways is a sign of considerable artistic power of composition. The north face is similar to the south with abstract patterns.

Scholars of early British and European art have long debated how such outstanding work came to such a remote spot 1,300 years ago. Outstanding art of this maturity and sophistication does not appear out of a sculptural vacuum; its sources and development can generally be traced. At the time that the cross was made, around AD 700, two quite different Christian missionary campaigns were taking place in Britain. Firstly, the mission of St Augustine, starting with his arrival in Kent from Rome in AD 597, had progressed rapidly northwards so that the Saxon kingdom of Northumbria within which Bewcastle lay had accepted Christianity by AD 620, explaining the possible

reference to King Alcfrith on the cross. Secondly, the Irish monk St Columba had brought Celtic monasticism to the island of Iona off the west coast of Scotland about AD 560. By 650 this monastery was sending missionaries southwards to England, often at the request of Northumbrian and other Saxon kings. Ionan monks with a distinctive Irish cultural background would have passed through Bewcastle on their way south. Now Irish monasticism derived from the south of France as Christian Celts travelled between the two countries. These monasteries in the south of France in turn can be traced back to the early Coptic church in Egypt and scholars have identified Coptic influence in the iconography of the Bewcastle cross. Northumbria, therefore, was a melting pot of the Roman and Celtic churches and the influence of both their cultures can be seen in this remarkable cross.

The cross now appears to be the only Saxon monument on the site but it can hardly have been made to stand here entirely alone. No part of the adjacent church is Saxon (see below) but two pre-Conquest artefacts have been found: a gravestone and a font-like object. Furthermore, the south face of the cross has a sundial, minus its gnomon, about half way up. This suggests that in AD 700 there might have been a small community of monks here who would have needed the time for the celebration of the daily offices of the church.

So the first foreign arrivals at Bewcastle were part of a military campaign and the second, about five hundred years later, were part of a peaceful religious campaign. Yet another set of foreigners arrived just another five hundred years later when William Rufus, son of William the Conqueror, built a castle here as part of his campaign to force the Scottish kings to submit to his rule. Astonishingly it too was built within the Roman fort. This castle was replaced by another in the early fourteenth century as English–Scottish wars continued. It was built in a corner of the Roman fort in order to utilise two of the Roman ditches as part of its outer defences. Its ground plan is a square about ninety feet by ninety and the ruins still rise to about thirty feet.

The little church alongside the cross was built about 1220, as shown by the Early English Gothic windows at the east end. The rest was substantially rebuilt in the eighteenth and nineteenth centuries. It is beautifully maintained outside and inside and used for regular weekly services. Adjacent to the south side of the churchyard is the substantial eighteenth-century former rectory. A farmhouse lies between the church and the castle and there are just three other cottages nearby. These few buildings form the only communal centre of the parish, clustering together at the middle of a shallow protective bowl of low encircling hills from which isolated farmhouses look down upon them.

It is remarkable that this place now so remote and insignificant has been the point of intersection of several lines of English history, military, ecclesiastic and artistic. Today it lives quietly, welcoming a steady trickle of visitors to a work of art unequalled in its time in Europe. Its landscape and its history make it a truly magical place – but bring a good map with you on your journey.

ACCESS

The cross is accessible at all times. The church is open every day. There is access to the castle during daylight hours (no attendant). Guidebooks for all these are available.

BELOW, LEFT The little parish church serves a far-flung community of farms and cottages. The east end is early thirteenth century, the rest was rebuilt in the eighteenth and nineteenth centuries. The cross can be seen immediately to the right of the church.

BELOW, RIGHT The east window of the church has a modern stained glass representation of Christ as seen in the west face of the cross (see page 17).

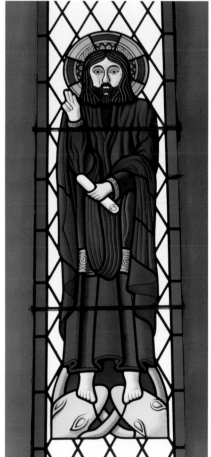

THE PRIORY CHURCH OF ST MARY MAGDALENE, LANERCOST, CUMBRIA

SURVIVAL AND RUIN IN THE SHADOW OF HADRIAN'S WALL

The interior of the ruined east end looking into the chancel from the south transept.

The nave and north aisle of the priory church were the only parts to survive the dissolution of the priory by Henry VIII in 1536.

Lanercost is a scattered settlement of farms and cottages without any clearly defined centre, just a few hundred yards south of Hadrian's Wall. The land here is not as open as elsewhere in this border country because the nearby River Irthing has cut a narrow valley through the surrounding low wooded hills. The Roman wall built in the years after AD 120 still makes its presence felt on the approach to Lanercost even when it cannot actually be seen. At junctions in the local network of minor roads, signposts direct travellers to military sites such as forts, mile castles and turrets and to domestic buildings, temples, shrines and monuments reflecting the everyday life of those who manned the wall.

In the early Middle Ages a sheltered and secluded place like this, adjacent to a river, was an ideal place for the site of a monastery. In 1155 Henry II granted lands

A medieval gateway frames the approach to the church. The west front beyond was completed in c.1220 in the Early English Gothic style.

in the area to Sir Hubert de Vaux. In 1166 his son Robert, who had succeeded him, gave some of these lands and a generous endowment for a house of Augustinian (or Austin) canons. The order derives its name from St Augustine, Bishop of Hippo in North Africa (340–430). He did not found the order but when its rule was formulated in the early Middle Ages it was based on advice he gave in a letter written to a group of religious women. The order was introduced into England about 1095 and grew rapidly to over two hundred houses by 1300. These houses were generally known as priories rather than abbeys because of their relatively small size. Unlike Benedictine, Cistercian and Carthusian monks, the priests of the order had a degree of freedom to leave their priories to minister among the laity. As a result they were known as canons (men living under a rule). The foundation at Lanercost in the far north of England in the mid-twelfth century shows how quickly and with what energy the Normans colonised the whole of the country and how deeply influenced they were by the ideals of the monastic life.

The exterior of the ruined east end of the church consisting of chancel and transepts. It is built of local New Red Sandstone.

The church was started in c.1175, which was near the end of the period of Norman or Romanesque architecture, and was finished in c.1220 when the Early English Gothic style was well established. There are traces of Norman work in the earliest, eastern, parts of the church but otherwise the church is in the latter style characterised by its tall, narrow lancet windows and its rib-vaulted roofs. The church is rather an austere building relatively free of ornament but two of the most characteristic Early English decorative motifs – dogtooth and stiff-leaf – appear in a few places in archways and the capitals of piers. Like all great monastic churches it has a cruciform plan of chancel, two transepts and a nave with one (north) aisle only. There is a low, plain tower over the crossing. The cloister with all its surrounding domestic buildings for the canons lies as usual on the south side of the church. Both church and cloister are built of a lovely pink New Red Sandstone.

The priory was never a large establishment, probably never exceeding twenty canons. During the thirteenth and fourteenth centuries the life of such a small community in a remote part of England should have been a peaceful one. Unfortunately for the canons, the priory was situated in a medieval 'war zone' where there were continual border battles between the English and Scottish kings as the former attempted to bring Scotland under their overlordship and the armies of the latter attempted to loot and plunder as much English land and property as they could. The priory was raided and sacked a number of times by the Scots under William Wallace and King David II. On their own side the canons were obliged to entertain Edward I (the 'Hammer of the Scots') on two occasions during his campaigns. The repair of damaged buildings and the hospitality provided to visiting royalty and barons were expensive and forced the canons into heavy debt during the last two hundred years of the priory's existence.

In 1536, the priory was 'dissolved' by Henry VIII (who also had his Scottish wars). As one of the poorer religious houses, with an income of less than £200 per annum, it was one of the first to go. Henry's Dissolution of the Monasteries was primarily a money-making exercise to finance his Scottish and French wars as well as a lavish lifestyle. Lanercost priory and its estates were sold to Sir Thomas Dacre whose father lived at nearby Naworth Castle (whose later inhabitants were responsible for the next church on our journey). The single, north aisle of the church was walled off from the rest and continued in use as a parish church. The rest of the church, although it became roofless, was relatively well-preserved with the walls maintaining their full height. Dacre converted the west range of the cloister to a mansion for himself. His descendants lived there until 1716 when the line died out. The remainder of the claustral buildings fared badly, used as a stone quarry by local farmers for barns, sheds and walls. In 1740 some restoration of the site was achieved when the parish decided to extend the area of the church in use by re-roofing the nave, walling up its eastern arch into the ruined crossing area beyond and then reconnecting it to the north aisle by removing the partition wall installed 200 years previously. This arrangement has been retained ever since.

Visitors today approach the priory through the remains of a medieval gateway to the west, from which they have a beautiful framed view of the west end of the church with its fine set of three Early English lancets and doorway below. A driveway crosses a field to the buildings. The interior of the present church is, as we have seen, only the western half of the canons' church but nonetheless it is an impressive space, taller than it is wide. Above the arcade between nave and north aisle there is a clerestory with its own arcaded wall passage running in front of it, the sort of architectural enrichment seen only in greater churches. Inevitably there is a sense of oddness here: there is no proper chancel area or south aisle to balance the north. Moreover, the tall south wall of the nave is quite windowless below because it forms the north walk of the cloister on the other side. There is some excellent glass in the north aisle lancets, although their tall narrow shape restricts the composition available to the artists. There are windows by William Morris and Edward Burne-Jones dating from 1875–96 (pages 26–7) and one from the early twentieth century by Evie Hone of the Irish school of glassmakers.

After leaving the church visitors can make their way round to the ruined east end to see the chancel and its chapels, the transepts and their aisles, and the crossing tower above. These parts stand up to their full height and they are a good example of Early English Gothic at its best, noble in its proportions and dignified in its restrained decoration. There are a number of monuments to the Dacre family, some of them from before the Dissolution. The most impressive, in New Red Sandstone as elsewhere, commemorates Sir Thomas Dacre K.G., who died in 1525. Its sides have the arms of Dacre and those of his wife. Around the cloister the west side rises to the greatest height because this is where the post-Reformation Dacres created a family mansion. It too, however fell into ruin after they left in 1716. In the south range little of the refectory remains but beneath it is the most impressive survival of the domestic quarters. This is the cellarium used for the storage of food, beer and other materials. It consists of two parallel aisles separated by an arcade of nine bays, which supports a rib-vaulted roof. Those familiar with the much larger structure at Fountains Abbey, North Yorkshire, will see the resemblance between the two.

So here is survival and ruin, both on an impressive scale in surroundings that have always been beautiful, but not always as idyllically peaceful as now.

ACCESS

The church is open every day, with a stall selling books, souvenirs and local produce. The ruined part of the church and the cloister buildings are cared for by English Heritage, who charge a small entrance fee, open most days from spring to autumn.

The tomb of Sir Thomas Dacre in the south transept. A prominent local landowner, he died in 1525.

The thirteenth-century cellarium below the canons' refectory was used for the storage of food, beer, etc.

ST MARTIN, BRAMPTON, CUMBRIA

A VICTORIAN JEWEL BOX OF MAGNIFICENT STAINED GLASS

Brampton is a small town or large village about ten miles northeast of Carlisle. Until recently the main road between Carlisle and Hexham passed through the town but now, happily for all concerned, it has been re-routed about a mile away. Shops, pubs, hotels and other businesses are grouped around a square in the centre, which is always an advantage in a small town, both visually and practically. There are also smaller squares and enclaves near by, all linked by a network of narrow streets. Most of the sturdy-looking red sandstone buildings are from the seventeenth, eighteenth and early nineteenth centuries, all in harmony with each other and the surrounding countryside. The town has charm and character of a typical North Country kind, quite different from the softer prettiness of southern villages.

The late-nineteenth-century parish church is the creation of a number of outstanding men of the time: an architect, artists and craftsmen – and a wealthy patron. It will be best to turn first to them and their ideas before seeing how the latter came to fruition in the church. William Morris (1834–96) was the son of a successful businessman who had homes in London and Essex. As a youth and young man Morris had artistic leanings and he spent much of his time touring the village churches of Essex. He fell in love with the beauty and the quality of the craftsmanship that he saw and it left a lasting impression on him. He loved the buildings themselves; the carving of the stonework; the medieval tiles; the woodwork of roofs, screens and benches; the metalwork and the stained glass. He admired the same sort of craftsmanship that he saw in the old farmhouses and cottages of the area. He contrasted this with the ugliness of their mass-produced contemporary counterparts, machine-made in factories by bored and dispirited employees who played little or no part in their design or construction. He became convinced that things of beauty and lasting quality could be produced only by craftsmen whose pride and joy in their skills were infused into the hand-made things they created. He was later to become a founding father of the Arts

The northwest view of the church built of red sandstone in 1874 in a 'free' version of the Gothic style.

and Crafts Movement, which was based on these ideas, and he was also the inspiration of other organisations that tried to improve design, craftsmanship and the love of art. He believed that the creation of craft guilds of the type common in the Middle Ages would enable furniture and other craft goods to be available not only to the rich but to all classes of society. This view of the Middle Ages was no doubt idealised, as was the idea that quality hand-crafted furnishings could be produced at prices that working class people could afford – hardly true even today with higher living standards. It is interesting to note in a book about churches that Morris was the founder of the Society for the Protection of Ancient Buildings (SPAB), set up to try to stop the wholesale and damaging 'restorations' of old churches referred to in the Introduction.

At Oxford University he met Edward Burne-Jones (1838–98), a fellow divinity student. They became lifelong friends and working partners. Under the influence of Morris, Burne-Jones became interested in art but while at that time Morris was primarily interested in architecture, Burne-Jones turned to painting. After leaving university Morris became apprenticed to G.E. Street, a leading architect, and Burne-Jones became apprenticed to Dante Gabriel Rossetti (1828–82). In 1848 Rossetti had been one of the founding members of the Pre-Raphaelite Brotherhood together with John Everett Millais and William Holman Hunt. The name of this 'brotherhood' derived from their belief that from the time of the Italian painter Raphael (1483–1520) the art of painting had become debased by a desire for grandeur, showiness and false effects, later to be known as the 'grand manner'. The brotherhood believed that this had become ingrained in the aesthetic canons of the national art academies of Europe ever since. They considered that 'truth' had been sacrificed to beauty and advocated a return to a style of greater naturalness and realism that was characteristic of Italian painters of the fourteenth and fifteenth centuries before Raphael. The paintings of the Pre-Raphaelites had a sharply focussed almost photographic quality expressed in bright colours. It was admired by some and hated by others. Burne-Jones was greatly influenced by the Pre-Raphaelite, ideas. Following them he favoured romanticised medieval and mythological subjects.

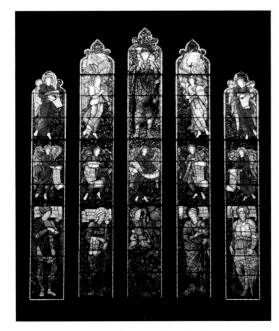

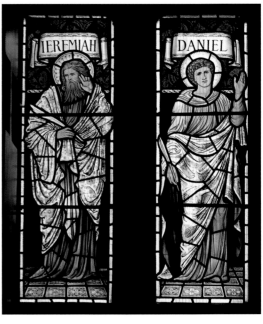

The east window, the largest in the church, was regarded by Edward Burne-Jones as one of the best he designed. It shows Christ the Good Shepherd (top, centre) with angels and saints.

East window detail: Dorothy and George Howard, patrons of the church, are commemorated by St Dorothy (left) and St George, in shocking pink.

The Old Testament prophets Jeremiah and Daniel.

In his own words he saw a picture as a 'beautiful romantic dream'. His pictures were peopled with almost impossibly fine-featured, nobly chivalrous men and divinely beautiful women. It was ironic that this originated in a movement dedicated to realism. After their apprenticeships Burne-Jones was to remain a painter, illustrator and designer but Morris turned away from architecture as such to an interest in a variety of associated crafts, dismayed by the lack of good craftsmen in every branch of furnishing. Thus he became skilled in the making of furniture, glass, tiles, wallpaper and soft furnishings such as carpets, curtains and upholstery. He founded a firm that eventually became known as Morris & Co., based on the medieval trade guilds in which enthusiastic and dedicated men developed their skills. Pevsner wrote that 'this event marks the beginning of a new era in Western art'. The company thrived, partly because of the quality of the very varied products it made and partly because of the business acumen of Morris. Burne-Jones became a member of the company, producing some superb designs, particularly for stained glass and tapestries. Morris & Co. had no defined policy as regards 'style', but because of their admiration for the Middle Ages their work was medievalising in character. There was only one full-time professional architect closely associated with Morris & Co. This was Philip Webb (1831–1915), who like Morris had trained in the office of G.E. Street and shared their Arts and Crafts ideals.

Throughout Victoria's reign new churches were being built at an unprecedented rate, especially in cities and their expanding suburbs. For these stained glass was needed in large quantities. Since the beginning of the nineteenth century and the Gothic Revival in architecture some outstanding stained glass designers had emerged, including the 'father' of the Gothic Revival, A.W.N. Pugin. However, the bulk of the glass produced was poor. The subject matter was sentimental and the designs were weak and over-detailed as though they were paintings on canvas. The colours were dull with much use of muddy olive greens and yellows. Like most other crafts at the time production was on a factory line basis. Morris & Co. were to make the most important and individual contribution to transforming the design (Burne-Jones) and manufacture (Morris) of stained glass in the nineteenth century. Burne-Jones did the drawings (or cartoons) in monochrome in the Pre-Raphaelite manner with his angels and saints having that ethereal, romantic quality so beloved by the brotherhood. Morris chose the colour scheme and supervised the cutting and assembling of the glass pieces. In the latter process he realised, as the medieval glass-makers had done, the importance of the lead strips (calms), which hold together the small individual pieces of glass that depict such things as the heads, shoulders and arms of the figures in the picture. The calms create sharp black defining outlines and are an essential characteristic of medieval glass, so different from a painting on paper or the glass painting technique of the eighteenth century (page 85).

We can now return to Brampton church, which is an outstanding monument to the Arts and Crafts Movement. In the middle of the nineteenth century the town was without a proper church. The town originally grew up in the twelfth century on a site about a mile away where there was a small Norman church. Some time later the settlement shifted to the present position but this building continued to serve as the parish church. The isolated site became known as Old Brampton. (There is nothing there today except the old church and a large farmhouse but it is a place of enviable tranquility amid gloriously panoramic scenery, well worth visiting.) Because of the distance between the old church and the new town various not very satisfactory chapels-of-ease replaced each other over the years within the town. In 1874 it was decided that this was no longer satisfactory. The town was fortunate in this respect to be within the fiefdom of the Howard family, Earls of Carlisle, whose ancestral seat at Naworth Castle is a few miles away. The family inherited the castle when they married into the Dacre family in the late sixteenth century, a family whose role at Lanercost church was described in the previous chapter. (The Howards of Castle Howard in North Yorkshire, famous from television's *Brideshead Revisited*, are a junior branch of the family.) Members of the Naworth Castle family financed the building of a new church at Brampton when they commissioned Philip Webb as architect, a man who had worked for them on previous projects. He could design in any style but generally favoured 'free' forms of Gothic of any period without ever attempting mere imitation of the medieval. The church he designed for Brampton reflects that preference and individualism. It consists of chancel, nave, two aisles and a west tower with a small lead spire. This description is a considerable simplification because the plan is one of some complexity. There is much inventiveness in all the details. It is built of the region's New Red Sandstone.

The principal purpose of this visit to Brampton is to see the magnificent collection of stained glass by Morris & Co., i.e. by Burne-Jones and Morris, inserted between 1880 and 1895. Webb had suggested to the Howards that the firm should be employed to insert the glass in his church, regarding them, rightly, as the leading glaziers of the time. George Howard, ninth Earl of Carlisle, was in any event a patron of the Pre-Raphaelites and a personal friend of Burne-Jones and Morris. The latter in his turn was always especially keen to have his glass inserted in a contemporary church rather than in a medieval one because he was always fearful that in the latter case it would be part of one of the restorations that, as an SPAB man, he deplored. The glass was not placed here as part of one single overall scheme but gradually over a period of about fifteen years. What the glass lacks as a unified scheme it gains in variety of subject matter. Like all of the firm's work it has a beautiful, glowing, jewel-like quality. It is all figurative glass, much of it commemorative in purpose, mainly for members of the Howard family. There are fourteen windows (many of them with several separate lights) by Morris & Co. but it is possible to show only a selection of them here. The largest single composition is the five-light east window. In the top tier is the Good Shepherd at the centre and angels left and right. Below is a row of angels and below that again a row of saints. The latter include St Dorothy and a remarkable St George in various shades of pink.

Three allegorical figures represent the three cardinal virtues of Faith, Hope and Charity.

They commemorate Dorothy and George Howard. The Old Testament is represented by the prophets Jeremiah and Daniel. The 'paradise window' is a rose window of angels (page 125). A window in the chancel has allegorical female figures representing Hope, Faith and Charity. Little Bessie Howard, who died aged four months in 1883, when infant mortality was high, is commemorated by no fewer than three windows. One of them shows children of the New Testament and their parents. Hundreds of churches have one or two windows by Morris & Co.; only a small handful have a complete collection like this, something that only the richest of patrons could afford.

When Edward Burne-Jones and William Morris died at the end of the nineteenth century a few of their followers continued their style and ideals into the twentieth century, notably Christopher Whall (page 76), but essentially their art died with them so the years of their work represent a unique era in the art of stained glass making. Fortunately the last third of the twentieth century has seen a notable resurgence in the art with a dozen or more practitioners creating pictorial and abstract glass of the highest quality in cathedrals and parish churches (pages 68 and 119). Invariably they use deep glowing colurs that owe much to Burne-Jones and Morris. Clearly the desire to beautify the House of God continues.

ACCESS

The church is generally open in the summer months. There are guidebooks and other literature on sale.

THE CHURCH OF ST NINIAN
AND THE CASTLE, BROUGHAM, CUMBRIA

WITNESSES TO THE ENERGY AND AMBITIONS OF
A REDOUBTABLE SEVENTEENTH-CENTURY COUNTESS

About a mile from the nearest road this is the first glimpse that visitors have of St Ninian's church, totally alone among the Cumbrian fells.

The architectural details of the exterior tell of the mid-seventeenth century.

The village of Brougham is about two miles southeast of Penrith on the road to Appleby. The road passes through the same exhilaratingly open, gently hilly countryside characteristic of the Scottish borders, although when travelling eastwards the much higher ridge of the Pennines can be seen in the distance, and when westwards the high Cumbrian mountains. The road now bypasses the village but its castle is a prominent landmark for travellers. Like so many of its kind it is now ruined but it is a very substantial and magnificent ruin. In places it rises through four storeys to a height of about eighty feet. Many of the numerous rooms and stairways inside are still roofed and can be seen by visitors. It was built during the reign of Henry II (1154–89) as a royal fortress in a troublesome part of his kingdom endangered by the Scots who were not then under English rule. In the late thirteenth century the castle passed by marriage to the Clifford family, Earls of Cumberland, great landowners in the area about whom more presently.

Continuing for about a mile in the direction of Appleby only very observant motorists will notice a field gate set back a little from the road on the northern side and beside it a small wooden signpost pointing away across the fields. There is just room to park a car here and to see that the sign directs walkers to 'Ninekirks'. This is a local name for the church of St Ninian, again reflecting the proximity to Scotland since St Ninian lived and worked as a missionary in the fourth century in the south of the country.

The twelfth-century castle at Brougham, one of several owned by Lady Anne Clifford, was restored by her in 1650 as her principal residence.

There is no building in sight but a rough track leads across the fields and shortly comes to the side of the River Eamont, a tributary of the River Eden, whose fast-flowing waters have cut a deep bed that reveals the local New Red Sandstone in its banks. This is a lovely warm-coloured sandstone, particularly in bright sunlight. As you continue on this fine walk, perhaps starting to wonder about any church, the track rises slightly and from the brow of the incline there is a remarkable sight. About 400 yards ahead, a low, ground-hugging church of red sandstone lies in the middle of a field surrounded by a fenced, overgrown graveyard with not another building in sight. A small bellcote at the west end gives the building more the appearance of a chapel than of a church. Closer up, among the eighteenth- and nineteenth-century gravestones, it can be seen that the architecture is all of one style and that the round-headed windows under square hood-moulds and the priest's door into the chancel all tell of the mid-seventeenth century. There is now the moment of anxiety that all church explorers experience: will the heavy oak door be locked? Is it safe to leave a church open in this isolated position? In fact the church is open every day for twenty-four hours to welcome the few visitors who have managed to discover it.

Once inside it takes only a glance to see that this is somewhere special. Everything in the interior matches the mid-seventeenth century date outside. Structurally and in its furnishings it is clearly in the same untouched condition as in the year it was made. This is a remarkable survival given the love that the Victorian churchmen had for drastic 'restorations' to bring interiors into line with new ideas of liturgical practice. The interior is a single

rectangular room, the aisleless nave and the chancel having no structural division between them. Everything contributes to a sense of cool, calm dignity in which nothing is out of place. The floor is made of massive stone flags; everything else is either white or dark brown. The walls are rendered and limewashed, as is the ceiling. All else is wood: the smoothly planed box pews and the rougher timbers of the roof above. At the front of the church are two family pews much taller than the rest, of the so-called 'horse box' type with balusters in the upper part, twisted in the Jacobean way. The communion rails have the dumb-bell form of the later seventeenth century. The altar reredos, pulpit and the stone font are all of the same period. To one side of the studded oak door through which you entered there is a contemporary iron poor-box, in which the money drops down a tall pillar for the sake of security. Pilfering was then doubtless the same problem as now. Above it on the wall hangs an eighteenth-century funeral hatchment, which gives one of the few restrained splashes of colour to the interior. A funeral hatchment is a coat of arms painted on wood or canvas made on the death of a member of an aristocratic family, hung outside the house before the funeral before being transferred to the parish church afterwards. Some churches have up to a dozen of these hanging on their walls.

Most visitors will wonder why such a church was built in such a remote place, apparently for the first time in the seventeenth century. The period was not one of church building in England. The huge legacy of medieval churches and the religious strife following the Reformation for several generations saw to that. The answer to the question can be found in two features in the church: those high family pews which tell of someone of rank and the letters AP moulded in the plaster beside the altar, surrounded by a garland. The whole of the land around here, and much beyond, was the property of the Clifford family, Earls of Cumberland. The 3rd Earl, George Clifford (1558–1605), married Margaret Russell, daughter of the Earl of Bedford and they had a daughter, Lady Anne Clifford, born in 1590. The Earl left the countess some time after Anne's birth and thereafter mother and daughter had a particularly close relationship. At the age of nineteen Lady Anne married Richard Sackville, Earl of Dorset, who died in 1624. Her mother had died in 1616. She married secondly Philip Herbert, Earl of Pembroke and Montgomery, but he too died in 1650 leaving Anne a widow for the second time at the age of sixty. Neither of these marriages had been successful by her own account. Anne had been lonely and unhappy living in great houses so far from home.

LEFT, ABOVE The seventeenth-century interior is exactly as made for Lady Anne in 1650, creating an atmosphere of cool, calm dignity.

LEFT, BELOW The family 'horse box' pews of Lady Anne and her household.

RIGHT Alongside the dark oak door into the nave is a seventeenth-century pillar poor-box designed for security, and an eighteenth-century funeral hatchment.

By this time Henry Clifford, the 5th Earl of Cumberland, had died without male issue in 1643 and under the terms of her father's will Anne had inherited the vast estates of the Clifford family in Cumberland, Westmorland and Yorkshire. After the death of her second husband she travelled north to claim her property using the grandiloquent titles of Lady Anne Clifford, Dowager Countess of Dorset, Pembroke and Montgomery. At the age of sixty (then a greater age than now) a quiet retirement might have seemed in order but that was not in her nature. In the event she was to have twenty-six years of life remaining and she devoted it untiringly to two passionate causes. The first involved repairing or even rebuilding the family castles and the parish churches on her estates that had fallen into disrepair or near dereliction. Stone, brick and mortar were now the materials of her life. The second was based on an immense family pride and a preoccupation in claiming for herself through the courts several ancestral titles, mainly baronies subsidiary to the earldom that had accrued to the Cliffords over the centuries. Following the repair of her homes it became her custom to spend fixed times of the year at each of her six castles: at Brougham, Appleby, Brough, Pendragon, Skipton and Barden, the last two being in West Yorkshire. All this might imply an extravagant lifestyle. In fact she had a frugal personal way of life regarding food, clothing and travel. Much of her wealth not taken up by building operations was dispensed in charity and to friends and relatives. It must be remembered that all of this was taking place during one of the most troubled periods of English history: the conflict between Charles I and Parliament followed by the Civil War. Lady Anne was an outspoken supporter of the King against the Parliamentarians and of the High Church party against the puritans when it was a dangerous time for such outspokenness. So we get the picture of an extremely feisty old lady with prodigious physical energy and immense ambitions and willpower.

This is the person we should have in mind as we stand inside the remote and highly atmospheric little church among the Cumbrian fells. When she returned north in 1650 she found at Brougham a medieval church in poor condition. She wrote in her diary: 'It [Ninekirks] would in all likelihood have fallen down it was soe ruiness if it had not bin repaired by me.' The rebuilding (for such it was) was carried out in 1650–1 and has never been altered since, outside or inside, except for a small south porch added in the nineteenth century. A well-preserved seventeenth-century church is a very precious survival for the reasons already mentioned. The quality but quiet restraint of all the furnishings indicates a patron of wealth and good taste. They were designed to provide the simple dignified setting that high churchmen liked for the celebration of the liturgy at that time. We can now understand the reason for those two tall family pews at the front of the church used by Lady Anne and her household and for the garlanded letters AP with the date 1660. They stand for Anne Pembroke. She never failed to leave a discreet yet reasonably prominent reminder to posterity of her restorations of all her churches and castles. After a time in the church one becomes conscious of the absolute stillness here. No church in England can be more remote and secret. I have visited about 2,000 English churches and the one at Brougham remains among the ten most memorable because of its setting, its architecture, its furnishings and its associations with a remarkable lady. Whatever village was around the church originally in the Middle Ages has long since disappeared and the church was inevitably made 'redundant' several years ago. It is now in the care of the Churches Conservation Trust, a splendid organisation that looks after over 300 similar churches, often although not always as small and remote like this. The Trust maintains the fabric and the furnishings in perfect condition.

On the way back to the road, their cars and modern life, visitors might now in their minds see a little procession of no doubt black-robed ladies and their male attendants making their way on horseback or in carriages along the same track from Brougham castle to morning service at the church on Sunday mornings over 300 years ago.

Before leaving the parish of Brougham visitors can see one further and moving reminder of Lady Anne. On the main Penrith–Appleby road, between the castle and the track that leads to Ninekirks, there is the so-called Countess Pillar perched on an embankment high above the road. It was erected in 1656 by Lady Anne to commemorate the place where she had her last meeting with her mother forty years before when as Countess of Dorset she was returning south to her husband after a visit home. The monument is an octagonal pillar with a cubic top and a truncated pyramidal roof and finial. On the cube are armorial shields (never far from Anne's mind), a sundial and the inscription: 'A memorial of her last parting in this place with her good and pious mother Ye Right Honourable Margaret, Countess Dowager of Cumberland Ye 2nd April 1616 . . .'

Lady Anne is buried in Appleby church where a large but typically restrained monument has no effigy but a tall wall plate with inevitably again a large display of coats of arms of the Cliffords, Russells and the families into which they married. A few yards away is the monument to her mother, in this case with a recumbent effigy of the countess superbly sculpted in alabaster with her gilded coronet on her head.

Posterity must be grateful to Lady Anne Clifford for the architectural heritage she has left us. For those whose imagination has been caught by her life and work, a tour of all her castles and churches is well worthwhile, but it will take time – and the coverage of many miles.

ACCESS

The church is open all day every day. The Churches Conservation Trust provides a welcoming atmosphere with a guidebook and other literature.

ABOVE On the Penrith road is the Countess Pillar, on which Lady Anne commemorated her last meeting with her mother, the Countess of Cumberland, in 1616.

ABOVE, RIGHT The tomb of Lady Anne in Appleby church. Its huge array of coats of arms of the Clifford family and those that it married into indicate her passionate interest in her family lineage.

RIGHT The tomb of Lady Anne's mother, the Countess of Cumberland, a few yards from her own. Her superbly sculpted effigy includes her gilded coronet.

MARTINDALE, HAWKSHEAD AND CARTMEL FELL, CUMBRIA

THREE CHURCHES AMONG LAKES AND MOUNTAINS

This is an outdoor group portrait of three churches that have a number of things in common, principally that they are all surrounded by the most stunning scenery in England. They are all small rustic churches and, although not included in the illustrations here, their equally humble interiors are atmospherically lovable and interesting.

One of the main roads northwards through the Lake District runs along the west side of Lake Ullswater. From the north end of the lake another minor road runs down the east side ending in a cul-de-sac in the scattered hamlet of Martindale. The little church of St Martin was built tucked in below a fell in 1633, a simple rectangular building of local slate with only a small bellcote to show that it is a church. Inside, the Jacobean furnishings are mainly original. Unusually the benches face each other across the central space, collegiate style. A new church was built in 1880 closer to the houses and St Martin's is now used only for occasional services in summer.

The village of Hawkshead is at the northwest end of Esthwaite Water, close to the centre of the National Park. From the elevated churchyard perched above the rooftops of the houses below there are views of a five-mile chain of mountains to the north. Those who like the Lake District for its own sake should be warned that Hawkshead is no longer the attractive, typically Lakeland village that it once was. It has always attracted visitors, partly for its beautiful setting, partly for its associations with William Wordsworth who attended the still existing late-sixteenth-century grammar school here from 1777–83 and Beatrix Potter who lived near by. By the 1960s tourism was growing but was still on a scale that the village

LEFT St Martin, Martindale, was built beneath a fell in 1633 to serve a remote little community close to Lake Ullswater. It retains its original furnishings.

RIGHT The late medieval church of St Michael, Hawkshead, is perched above the rooftops of the houses of this much visited village with panoramic views of the mountains beyond. The young William Wordsworth worshipped here while attending the grammar school immediately below it.

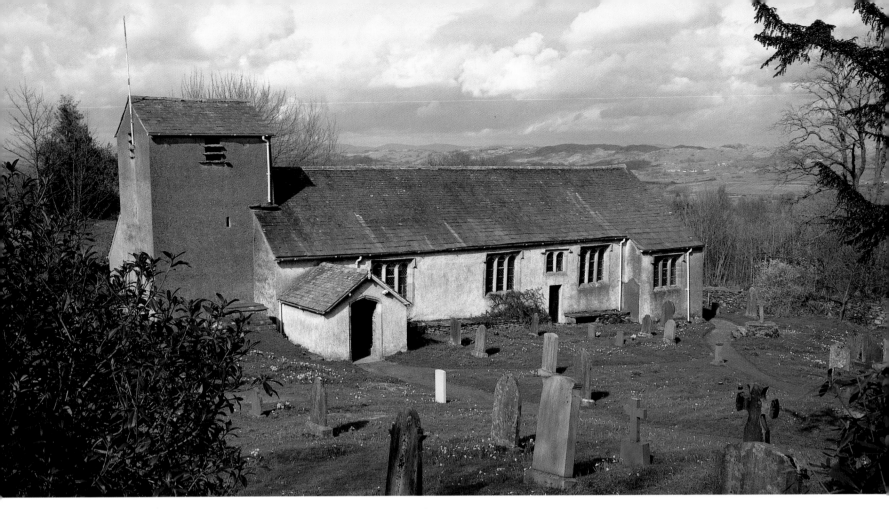

St Anthony, Cartmel Fell, is a lonely and remote church built in 1505 among the hills south of the lakes, crouching on the ground as though for protection.

could absorb. Since then the continued exploitation of tourism has been ruthless. Large, almost department-like stores have been purpose built, selling 'Lakeland' clothing and tourist bric-à-brac. There are cafés and tearooms to saturation point. Car parks and toilets cover a large part of the village. Towns like Windermere, Kendal and Keswick can to some extent survive this kind of thing; a village cannot. It is beyond comprehension how the famously strict planning laws of the National Park have allowed it. Fortunately the parish church of St Michael survives serenely above all this both literally and figuratively, a short steep climb behind the main street. It is a plain sturdy church built in the late medieval or post-medieval period. Sturdy too is the only way to describe the interior. Pevsner was 'baffled' by the huge, shapeless, whitewashed piers and arches but found the interior nonetheless 'engaging'.

Cartmel Fell, in a different world from the tourism of Hawkshead, is very isolated and very lonely. Only people who know of this place and who have the perseverance necessary to find it will ever reach here. Cartmel Fell is a group of low hills at the southern end of the Lake District. There is no village or even a hamlet, just a scattered community of farms and cottages. Despite its name it is about eight miles northeast of the well-known village of Cartmel (pages 37-41) and quite difficult to find, almost impossibly so if it were not for the signposts to 'The Church' at the lane junctions on the last mile or so. The only building within sight of it is the former nineteenth-century primary school, now a parish hall. The church was built in 1505 as a chapel of ease for the distant parish church at Cartmel. Like so many of its kind it is a low building crouching on the ground for protection from the weather at this elevation. Even the west tower hardly rises above the nave roofline. What it does share with Hawkshead is the magnificent panoramic view to the mountains to the north. The church has an attractively rustic interior with family pews made out of former chancel screens after the Reformation for local squires. There is an especially interesting stained glass window of 1505 behind the altar showing a Crucifixion linked to the administration of the seven sacraments. If you stay here for an hour or two you are unlikely to see another soul – a different world indeed.

When touring or hiking among the lakes lovers of English churches will find much of interest in addition to its famous scenery.

ACCESS

The three churches are generally open each day.

ST MARY AND ST MICHAEL, CARTMEL, CUMBRIA

A PRIORY CHURCH THAT DOMINATES A VILLAGE

Cartmel is many people's favourite village in south Cumbria, as witnessed by the number of visitors between spring and autumn. However it is not a number so large as to overwhelm and destroy because Cartmel has not sold its soul to commercialism as Hawkshead has (pages 35–6). The village gives its name to the Cartmel peninsula at the southern end of the Lake District, which is surrounded by Morecambe Bay. The mountains further north have given way to low fells and farmland; indeed for a mile or two around the village the land is quite flat. Cartmel is compactly centred on a small square that is more attractive visually and socially than a ribbon village spread out along a long high street. The area lies on a formation of Carboniferous limestone, the same that underlies the Yorkshire Dales to the east, and as a result many of the older village buildings reflect this geology in their attractive silver-grey stonework except where it has been rendered and limewashed. The little square is lined with buildings of the seventeenth and eighteenth centuries: cottages, some

The architecture of the former priory church shows the evolution of styles during three hundred years of the Middle Ages. The low crossing tower with two stages arranged diagonally to each other is a very recognisable feature.

grander houses, two old inns and a homely, traditional village shop. There is one building, however, much older than these – a big medieval gatehouse with an archway over one of the narrow streets that lead into the square. Another of these streets bridges a fast-flowing little river on its way into the square. It is as charming a village centre as anywhere in England.

The gatehouse is connected with the one building that has always dominated Cartmel, physically, historically and socially – its great church. In 1188 William Marshall, Earl of Pembroke, founded a priory here for Augustinian canons and the village grew up around it, a home for its domestic servants, agricultural workers on its estates and the people involved in the trade that it created. This priory survived quietly for about 350 years, apparently never much involved in national affairs, until Henry VIII dissolved it in 1537 along with all the others of its kind. The canons' domestic quarters have disappeared entirely. The church, however, has survived in its entirety but only by a series of lucky escapes and the intervention of generous benefactors. It was saved initially at the Reformation when the villagers successfully claimed a 'parochial right' under the terms of the Act of Dissolution by showing that the church was used by the parish as well as by the canons. However, after that the villagers used only the south aisle of the chancel for their services, that no doubt being more than large enough. Within a hundred years the rest of the church had become extremely dilapidated and in 1620 George Preston, a local landowner of nearby Holker Hall, arranged a co-operative effort between himself and the villagers to effect a complete restoration of the whole building. In the eighteenth century, an age notoriously neglectful of its churches, it again deteriorated. It was again rescued in the nineteenth

LEFT The four massive early Gothic arches of the crossing area.

ABOVE RIGHT The chancel is separated from its aisle by an arcade that is Norman in its lower parts and Early English Gothic in the upper.

RIGHT The north aisle leading from the nave into the transept and the chancel beyond that is early Gothic of c.1220.

The tomb of the first Lord Harrington, who died in 1347, and his wife. The effigies are surmounted by a canopy with the sumptuously ornate forms of the Decorated Gothic style.

Detail of the Harrington tomb. Christ shows the wounds on His hands to the world.

century by the Cavendish family, Dukes of Devonshire living at Chatsworth House in Derbyshire. A cadet branch of the family had become parishioners, having bought and rebuilt George Preston's Holker Hall.

As a result of all this the church today is happily much as the canons had known it. It consists of a chancel with aisles, north and south transepts, a short aisled nave and a crossing tower. The latter is a strange, disproportionately low, two-storey structure, the upper stage of which is set at forty-five degrees to the lower. Pevsner found it 'structurally dubious but entertaining'. Students of architectural history wishing to see good examples of the features of every style of medieval architecture from twelfth-century Norman Romanesque through each phase of Gothic, Early English, Decorated and Perpendicular, could do no better than come to Cartmel. When work started in 1190, late Norman architecture was still

current in most parts of England, although in the southeast the early Gothic style had been established at Canterbury cathedral and was rapidly spreading after its introduction from northern France. The early years of building at Cartmel were Norman. Ornate round-headed arches set within thick walls or above thick piers occur in a number of places, notably the grand south door and in the arcade separating the chancel from its aisles. After about three decades Early English Gothic had reached Cartmel in *c*.1220. Outside there are narrow pointed lancet windows; inside are the upper parts of the chancel and the whole crossing area, around which massive arches lead into the chancel and its aisles, the transepts and the nave and its aisles. Examples of typically sumptuous and sinuous Decorated Gothic forms of the late thirteenth and early fourteenth centuries are in the south chancel chapel, most notably in the tomb of the first Lord

The medieval canons' stalls (visible at the bottom of the picture) were given splendid screen backs in 1618. The nearly black oak columns are carved with vine trails and instruments of the Passion.

One of several modern works of art in the church. This is a metal statue of St Michael the Archangel, the co-patron of the church, by Josefina de Vasconcellos.

Harrington (d.1347) and his wife. It is 'one of the best of its date in England' (Pevsner). The two effigies are surmounted by a splendid tall canopy supported by decorated arches with figures of saints. On the top is a seated figure of Christ showing the wounds in His hands to the world. The Decorated style also appears in a number of aisle windows. The Perpendicular era of the late fourteenth and early fifteenth century is represented mainly by the enormous windows inserted to provide the ever-brighter interiors that characterised the later Middle Ages. The great east window is the size of a small tennis court.

There are many fine furnishings. Pre-eminent among them are the fifteenth-century canons' choir stalls in the chancel, their misericords carved with the usual grotesques and amusing scenes from everyday life. The showpieces here, however, are the backs to the stalls, a gift of George

Preston as part of his early-seventeenth-century restoration (above). The oak wood is now aged almost black. The columns separating each stall from its neighbours are carved with vine trails, among which are instruments of Christ's Passion. Much more recently the church has been beautified with a number of modern works of art. This is exactly as it should be, with each century contributing its own ethos to the ongoing living history of the church. Notwithstanding the periods of ruination and neglect in the past it is now in the twenty-first century a beautifully cared for church and obviously one much loved and prayed in.

ACCESS

The church is open every day. There is a bookstall. Holker Hall a few miles away is open to the public in the summer months.

ST MARY, KIRKBY LONSDALE, CUMBRIA

NORMAN ARCHITECTURE AT ITS MOST IMPRESSIVE

If Cartmel (pages 37–41) is many people's favourite village in south Cumbria, Kirkby Lonsdale is many people's favourite market town. From its centre, the Cumbrian hills, here lower and gentler than further north, are clearly visible in the near and far distance looking down the line of a street or wherever there is a gap in the houses. At the eastern end of the town the views are something special. From the parish churchyard the land drops down vertically to the River Lune, which has cut away the rock in its serpentine meander. The view to the north across the river was described by John Ruskin (1819–1900), writer on art, architecture and landscape, as 'one of the loveliest scenes in England – therefore in the world'. In honour of this advertisement for the town a viewing place in the form of a tall gazebo has been erected in the churchyard from where visitors can judge for themselves about 'Ruskin's View', as it is widely known. The town itself is a compact network of narrow streets that are still the same width as when they were laid out in a time of pedestrians, horses and horse-drawn carriages. Most of the buildings that let directly on to the pavements are seventeenth- and eighteenth-century, mainly cottages, small houses and numerous inns (I lost count). Occasionally a much grander eighteenth-century house manages to squeeze its way in between. Around the older centre, streets of sturdy looking Victorian terraced houses spread to the outer parts of modern housing but these are not extensive and do not intrude visually or otherwise on the older parts. All the buildings from before the twentieth century are grey stone; in fact Kirkby Lonsdale is a grey town. This is not as unattractive as it sounds. The stone is Carboniferous limestone whose colour varies from dark to silver-grey in pleasing variation. Sturdy vernacular architecture and spectacular fells around it are the town's claim as one of Cumbria's best.

The church is in a large churchyard entered through handsome wrought-iron gates and surrounded by houses on the south, east and west sides. As

'Ruskin's View' from the churchyard looks across the River Lune (foreground and mid-distance) to the Cumbrian fells beyond. Ruskin described it as 'one of the loveliest scenes in England'.

The church is long and low as though seeking protection on the ground from the elements. The exterior has features of all periods, Norman to late Gothic.

already described, the north side above the River Lune looks across to Ruskin's View. Hardly any better combination of landscape and architecture in any one place can be imagined. From outside, the low church looks interesting but not unusually impressive architecturally. It consists of chancel, aisled nave and a west tower. Most spectacular is the late Norman doorway below the latter, dating from *c*.1170 (see page 10). The Norman masons often made great effort on their doorways, conscious no doubt that this was the best opportunity to impress all those entering. In the usual Romanesque way the doorway is made up of a series of concentric round-headed arches that recede into the wall. The characteristically elaborate and varied carvings on each arch are now difficult to identify due to weathering of the stone. From this earliest part a continual evolution of building can be observed. The east end has thirteenth-century Early English Gothic lancet windows. Those in the chancel aisles are later Decorated Gothic while those of the nave aisles are Perpendicular Gothic of the fifteenth and sixteenth centuries. They reflect the increasing desire for more light as time went on in the Middle Ages.

The late Norman west doorway outside is a preview to the spectacular nave arcade inside which is some sixty years older. It is early Norman architecture at its most powerful and brutal. The arches between the massive piers seem quite narrow in comparison. The mouldings on the arches are all different. The piers have the incised spiral trellis-work that appears in a number of northern churches, derived from Durham cathedral. While all of this is impressive it is also rather oppressive, as in a medieval castle. Perhaps the Norman colonists felt themselves beleaguered in a strange country surrounded by natives who were not always friendly. The Norman state indeed had two arms, the secular and the ecclesiastical, and both are represented at Kirkby Lonsdale. The former is symbolised by the remains of the motte-and-bailey castle close to the high bank of the River Lune, an ideal defensive position.

Sometimes church explorers leave a town or village with only a memory of the church. At Kirkby Lonsdale they leave with three memories, the church, the town and the Cumbrian fells around them.

ACCESS

The church is open every day. There is a bookstall.

The spectacular early Norman nave arcade, *c*.1110. It exudes an almost brutal power, more akin to a castle than a church. The incised trellis-work on the piers derives from Durham cathedral.

THE PRIORY CHURCH OF ST MARY, LANCASTER, LANCASHIRE

ONCE IN A NORMAN CITADEL,
NOW IN A ROYAL DUCHY

Many towns in the early medieval period after the Norman Conquest were built on a hill. At that time a strong defensive position was important and the castle, which was needed almost as a matter of course, benefited from an elevated position for additional security. Lancaster is built on not one but on a group of adjacent hills. A tour of the city exercises the leg muscles as in few others. It also provides good views of one part from another, the more so as some of the most interesting and important buildings are on the hilltops. However, for those not fond of climbing there is plenty of good walking at sea level. The River Lune flows through the city centre to the eighteenth-century docks that made Lancaster an important inland port at that time. The Lancaster Canal also wends its way through the city. The paths alongside river and canal are full of interest whatever your tastes: architecture, archaeology or wildlife.

Architecturally what dominates the city centre now is the eighteenth century. Steep streets and little squares are lined with sturdy-looking three- and four-storey houses and public buildings of buff-coloured sandstone and in the way they face each other across narrow streets one is reminded more of Edinburgh than any English city. The building we have come to see, however, is much older than these. When the Normans reached Lancaster their building priorities were as usual twofold: a castle and a church, representing the two arms of the Norman state: the secular power invested in the king and the barons and the spiritual power invested in the clergy. It was naturally convenient for these two buildings to be as close together as possible within some kind of citadel providing mutual support. The Romans had chosen the rocky top of one of Lancaster's hills overlooking the River Lune as a castrum. It was an obvious and ideal place for the Norman citadel, making a grand statement to the countryside around. Castle and church are within yards of

East view from the top of the steps (bottom of picture) that end the steep climb to the church. It is a rebuilding of 1431 of an earlier church first built by the Normans.

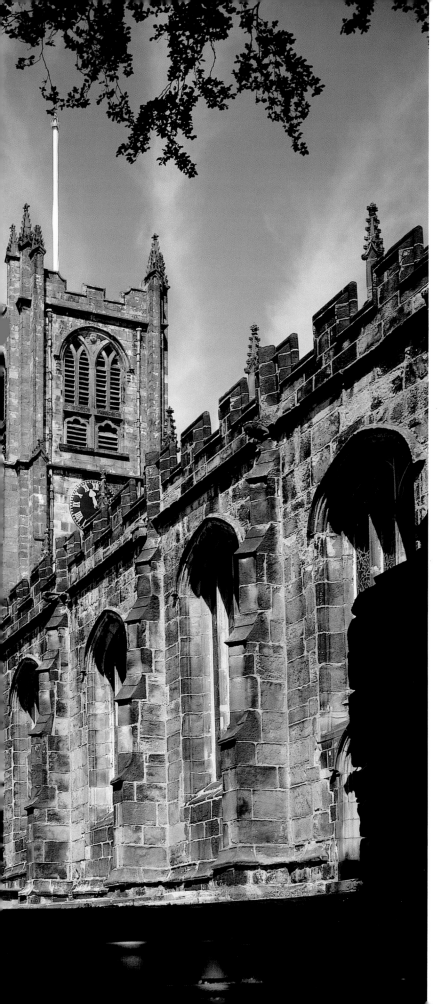

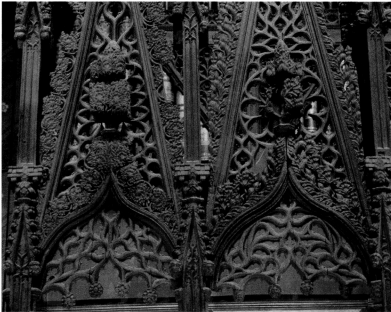

The mid-fourteenth century canopies of the monks' choir stalls have been described as the most luxuriant in England, characteristic of Decorated Gothic work of the time.

each other, an impressive sight. Because it is so much larger the castle is the more awesome. The church is by no means small but it is overshadowed by the sheer mass of its neighbour. The building of the two was part of the same campaign. After the Conquest, Roger of Poitou held the area from the Crown as Earl of Lancaster. In 1094 he founded a Benedictine priory as a cell (dependency) of Séez Abbey in Normandy, another example of the Normans' deep respect for and investment in monasticism. The keep of the first stone castle was begun some time after 1102.

There are no remains of the Norman church now visible above ground although excavations have revealed the foundations of the eastern parts. After that comes the Early English Gothic south porch. Otherwise the church is entirely Perpendicular Gothic. The rebuilding is attributed to the transfer of the priory from Séez to Syon Abbey outside London in 1431. The rebuilding consisted of a chancel with aisles, a nave with aisles and a west tower, the latter being rebuilt again in the eighteenth century. The golden yellow sandstone is as usual streaked with black. There are no traces of the priory's domestic buildings; the church survived the Dissolution of the Monasteries because it was also a parish church.

Inside 'the furnishings are plentiful and rewarding', according to Pevsner. Pride of place goes to the choir stalls used by the monks. Their canopies are 'the most luxuriant in the country' (Pevsner again). They are carved all over with dense and intricate foliage. The pulpit of 1619 has two unusual carvings on top of the tester, a bible and a crown. These might be taken as symbols of the two authorities in the Church of England: God and the

ABOVE On top of the seventeenth-century pulpit are symbols representing authority in the Church of England: the bible for God and the crown for Queen as Duke of Lancaster.

ABOVE, RIGHT The royal arms of the House of Windsor represent the Queen as monarch and Supreme Governor of the Church of England.

RIGHT One of the three large brass chandeliers dated 1717.

Queen as its Supreme Governor. However, the significance of the crown goes further than that in Lancaster. It connects with the way in which Lancaster, in some ways a rather obscure city, gave its name to events during a long period of English history. In 1351 in the reign of Edward III the Earldom of Lancaster first held by Roger of Poitou was raised to a Dukedom, with Henry of Lancaster, a cousin of the King, as the 1st Duke. For a time thereafter the dukedom was held by a member of the royal family, passing to John of Gaunt, fourth son of Edward III. On his death in 1399 it passed to his son, King Henry IV, and from that time to this it has passed by right to the sovereign. Throughout the fifteenth century the descendants of John of Gaunt, Duke of Lancaster and the descendants of

The moving monument to Sybil Wilson who lies dying on a couch in 1773 aged six years, watched by her grieving parents.

his brother, Edmund, Duke of York, both claimed the throne of England in the Wars of the Roses, the red rose of Lancaster pitted against the white rose of York. The crown above the pulpit at Lancaster priory church represents Queen Elizabeth II not so much as Supreme Governor of the Church of England but as Duke of Lancaster. She last visited the church in 1999 to celebrate the sixth centenary of the royal dukedom. For the same reason the royal arms of the House of Windsor appear in the west gallery. Although earlier royal arms such as those of the Stuarts and Hanoverians are seen frequently in old churches, those of Windsor are seldom seen in parish churches other than here.

There are several large, elegant brass chandeliers in the church dated 1717. Strangely, all of the monuments in the church are post-medieval. They include a moving monument to Sybil Wilson, who died in 1773 aged six

years. The child lies dying on a couch, her grieving mother and father in Roman dress sit and stand near by.

On all sides of the pleasant churchyard the land drops steeply, emphasising how effective this site was as a citadel. To the west and the north there are particularly spectacular views across Morecambe Bay to the Cumbrian mountains. Immediately to the south of the churchyard the huge mass of the Norman castle looms high above the church, although much of it is due to additions in the late eighteenth and early nineteenth century when a shire hall, court and gaol were incorporated within it.

ACCESS

The priory church is open every day. There are a shop and café within the building. The castle is open most days with guided tours.

ST JOHN THE BAPTIST OLD CHURCH, PILLING, LANCASHIRE

FROZEN IN TIME SINCE THE TIME OF JANE AUSTEN

The last stage of the journey to the village of Pilling on the south side of Morecambe Bay is strikingly similar to the Lincolnshire fens, particularly if you come via Cockerham. Both are low-lying, flat, marshy coastal areas with fields bordered by drainage ditches or deeper and wider dykes. In Lancashire marshy land is known as a 'moss' and there are several named on maps of the local area. For those familiar with the distant views of the spires of the great Lincolnshire fen churches the resemblance is enhanced by the first sight of the spire of Pilling New Church some miles away. However, the panoramic views you have in this area include things not seen in the fens – high hills. To the north, as you approach the village, the Cumbrian mountains are clearly visible about twenty miles away across Morecambe Bay, while on the return journey facing east, the lower hills of the Forest of Bowland are about five miles away and another fifteen miles beyond them the high ridge of the Pennines closes off the horizon.

LEFT The church from the southeast. It was built in 1717 with the typically simple rectangular ground plan and clear glass windows of the early Georgian period.

BELOW The yew alley leading to the south door through the churchyard.

Pilling is a scattered-out village without a clear centre and with little in the way of picturesque or historic buildings except the one we have come to see. The village is part of the huge parish of Garstang about six miles away to the southeast. In the Middle Ages it had a chapel-of-ease, which was served by the monks of Cockersand Abbey about the same distance to the north. After the Reformation the chapel remained in use served by curates until the beginning of the eighteenth century, when the villagers decided it was too small and dilapidated. A new church was built in 1717. It is a reasonably large building whose ground plan is a simple rectangle without structural division between nave and chancel, both of which have large clear glass windows. The only access is a simple doorway without a portico and there is no tower, only a rather baroque looking little bell-cote at the west end. All of this is characteristic of Georgian churches for which finance was limited. The approach to the south door across the spacious churchyard is through a yew alley planted relatively recently, a charming feature. That the church's builders had only a rather rustic knowledge of classical architecture is evident in their treatment of this south door, which has pilasters divided from the arch above by rather odd capitals. There is a pretty sundial above the door dated 1756 with the admonitory inscription 'Thus eternity approacheth'. The church is built of red sandstone with contrasting grey sandstone for the window and door surrounds.

The church is no longer used for regular worship, something you would not be aware of outside but which of course becomes apparent as soon as you enter. There is a magical awareness of being transported back into another world and another society, for this is an interior that has been little altered, with the exception on one addition, since the year it was built. The large clear glass windows flood the church with light – the absence of any later insertions of stained glass is just one example of how the Victorians left this church alone. The walls are rendered and shine with fresh limewash. The floor has large stone flags. The seating consists mainly of very plain dark oak benches, although inevitably the social proprieties of the time had to be observed in the form of three rather higher box pews at the front on the north side. These would have been for the rector's family, the squire and perhaps some prominent landowner. At the east end, below a large window is a typical 'puritan' chancel arrangement. The altar is a plain 'holy table' surrounded on three sides by communion rails with handsome carved balusters. The Low Church wing of the Anglican church favoured this arrangement in place of the more usual single communion rail across the full width of the chancel. In this way the minimum of separation between minister and congregation was created. One must realise how far removed this is from the medieval arrangement of a long chancel projecting east beyond the nave and separated from it by a heavy rood screen where the liturgy was conducted almost out of sight of the congregation. The pulpit to the right of the chancel was originally a three-decker but at some time the lower clerk's deck was removed (page 12). The minister read the prayers and lessons

The interior from below the pulpit. Since 1717 it has been changed only by the addition of the two-sided gallery in 1813.

from the middle deck and preached from the upper deck. Behind on the wall are the royal arms of George I dated 1719 with the specifically Hanoverian part of the arms in the fourth quarter.

In 1813, just a hundred years after the church was built, it had become too small and it was decided to build a two-sided gallery that stretched not only across the west end but continued down the full length of the north side as well. It is supported on slender classical style columns. The roof had to be slightly raised to allow for this and to light the north gallery a row of lunettes (semi-circular windows) was inserted high up in the north wall. With the addition of this gallery the church could seat 350 people. That the gallery was not simply for hoi polloi (as the gallery in a theatre) is shown by the fact that some of the seating up here is in the form of box pews with the family names on the doors. It is an odd sensation today sitting or standing in one of those pews that are at the chancel end, looking immediately down rather than upwards at the top deck of the pulpit. It seems that at Pilling the gallery formed what in a theatre would be the royal circle; the box pews on the ground at the front obviously the orchestra stalls while the plain pews at the back formed the pit. I find it easy to

imagine people in Georgian dress seated crowded in this church, or later, in Regency times, the women in long crinolines and the men in wide trousers, long frock coats carrying stovepipe hats. The church was built at the time that Jane Austen's grandparents would have been born; the gallery was added a few years before her death. Down in the south of England she would have known and loved churches just as this still is.

By 1883 the population of the village had risen to over 1,600, about twice what it had been when the gallery was added in 1813. Once again, therefore, it was decided to build a substantial new church on a site just 200 yards to the north of the old one. A handsome building of some character and originality, it was designed by the distinguished northern firm of architects Austin and Paley in the Gothic Revival style. The original intention was to demolish the eighteenth-century church but fortunately this was not done. The result, however, was that the new church was given the same dedication as the old, so that Pilling has had since then an Old Church of St John the Baptist and a New Church of St John the Baptist. It is, of course, the spire of the latter that one sees on the approach to the village.

The 'puritan' chancel with holy table and three-sided communion rails.

Although some maintenance work was done on the Old Church in the years that followed, by 1989 it was in a near ruinous condition with parts of the roof missing. Thankfully, the Churches Conservation Trust (then known as The Redundant Churches Fund) assumed responsibility for its care and instigated major repairs and conservation work with total respect for the historical integrity of the building. The Old Church is now in excellent condition outside and inside. The Old Church shares the same churchyard as the New Church, which means that there is a steady trickle of visitors around the Old Church as they tend family graves. That has prevented any sense of isolation that the building might otherwise have acquired. Pilling Old Church is not great architecture and its fittings and furnishings are not great art or craftsmanship. Pevsner gives it just eight lines in his North Lancashire volume. What makes it memorable to the average visitor is the way in which it remains a time capsule of a church interior, a form of churchmanship and a rural society of three hundred years ago. All thanks to the Churches Conservation Trust.

ST JOHN THE BAPTIST
OLD CHVRCH PILLING

This church is cared for by
The Churches Conservation Trust.
Although no longer needed for regular worship,
it remains a consecrated building,
a part of England's history,
maintained for the benefit of this
and future generations.

For habitual church explorers the name of the Churches Conservation Trust on its characteristic stone plaque is always a pleasant sight. It guarantees an accessible church and a warm welcome.

ACCESS

Visitors may obtain the key from an address given on the church door at most reasonable hours. A church guidebook and other literature are available inside.

ST ANDREW, SLAIDBURN, LANCASHIRE

JACOBEAN AND GEORGIAN OPULENCE IN A RUSTIC SETTING

The village of Slaidburn is near the centre of the Forest of Bowland, which covers about 300 square miles of central Lancashire. Since Merseyside and Greater Manchester have been separated from the county the Forest of Bowland now occupies about a third of its area, a surprise to those who think that Lancashire is largely industrialised cities and mill towns. There is not a great deal of forest in Bowland but there is almost every other kind of landscape, upland and lowland. The hills of the uplands are spread over the whole area, many of them rising to nearly 2,000 feet. Their broad tops are treeless, heather-covered moors, wilderness areas to match anything in England. Lower down there is sheep grazing and grouse shooting. The lowlands are valleys formed by fast-flowing rivers, which have created well-wooded pastoral farmland. The centre of the forest is free from main roads; only narrow lanes link up its distinctively North Country sandstone villages. For travellers in car or on foot even a short journey can be one of contrasts: one moment they may be on high ground with views of five miles or more; a short descent and a few corners later they may be alongside a river among lush fields and woods.

This changing scenery will be seen on the way to Slaidburn. The small village is in a narrow valley formed by the River Hodder, which flows around the village green. Beyond the river plain the views are closed in by gently rising hills. The village is a single winding high street lined by sandstone cottages that let directly on to the pavement, a lovely ensemble of seventeenth- and eighteenth-century domestic architecture. Nothing has been intruded to mar its character, a natural and uncontrived character without any self-conscious 'olde worlde' prettiness or any outward show of affluent modernity.

The church is at the southern edge of the village with fields on three sides of the spacious churchyard. On the north side is a handsome former grammar school of 1717, exceptionally large for such a small village. It is now a primary school. As visitors approach any church that they specially want to see inside there are always questions in mind. Will it be open? If not will a key be available? Slaidburn gives the answer quickly. A notice on the churchyard gate says:

St Andrew's Welcomes Visitors
The Church Is Open ca. 9 a.m. till Dusk

And on the church door itself:
The Church Is Open
You Are Welcome

The church has a beautiful setting but it is not especially distinguished architecturally from the outside. The nave and the two aisles are rendered, which is not an asset visually. Only the stonework of the west tower is exposed, the same buff sandstone as the village houses but mixed, unexpectedly, with a little pink sandstone. The earliest visible features are fourteenth-century Decorated Gothic.

Neither would the interior be notable except for the sumptuous Jacobean and Georgian furnishings at the junction of the nave and chancel. There is no chancel arch; the division between them is defined by a tall, heavy, dark oak screen. This is where a medieval rood screen would normally be in a church. This, however, is unmistakably post-Reformation, Jacobean of c.1620. It was clearly built as a display of wealth rather than for any reasons

The church from across the fields. The village is to the left and the River Hodder flows behind the churchyard.

of piety. It has tapering square uprights that support a heavy cornice with open tracery. It is carved overall with vine trails, grapes and little heads. It is thought that the maker was the same as made similar screens at Wakefied Cathedral and St John's Church, Leeds. There are tall box pews on both sides of the screen, i.e. in both the chancel and the nave. The former were probably for the rector's family, the latter for the 'quality' of the parish. There are box pews to the sides of these in the aisles but it is noticeable that some social distinctions were being made here since the boxes are not as tall as in the nave. Elsewhere in the church there are simple benches.

An equally striking post-Reformation piece of furniture is the exceptionally large three-decker pulpit. The red velvet drapery on each of the three decks creates an especially opulent effect. With his parish clerk in the lower deck a bewigged and gowned clergyman would read the prayers from the middle deck. For the sermon – sometimes lasting an hour or more – he would ascend to the top deck. From this great height he could see the eyes (open or closed) of his whole congregation. There are several eighteenth- and early-nineteenth-century brass chandeliers, which create a brighter sense of opulence than provided by the dark oak elsewhere. The east window is filled with a large Adoration of the Magi of 1868. Its acid colours, particularly the reds are eye-catching in this relatively dark interior.

At Slaidburn it is probably true to say that the church, the village and the landscape all contribute equally to the enjoyment of the visit.

ACCESS

As indicated above the church is open all day, every day. Guide leaflets are available. Note: Until recently Slaidburn was in West Yorkshire and it will be found listed there in many architectural gazeteers such as Pevsner and Betjeman.

The Jacobean screen between chancel and nave is a heavy oak structure ornately carved overall.

The opulent three-decker pulpit from which sermons of prodigious length were preached in the eighteenth century.

ALL HALLOWS, GREAT MITTON, LANCASHIRE

FINE FAMILY MONUMENTS IN A DRAMATICALLY SITED CHURCH

The fourteenth-century church seen across the River Ribble at the edge of the Forest of Bowland.

Great Mitton is right at the southern edge of the Forest of Bowland. All of its 300 square miles is beautiful but in a varied way, either gently arcadian or spectacularly wild. From Great Mitton churchyard one can enjoy a marvellous meeting of both types of scenery. Great Mitton is a hamlet consisting of the church, a Jacobean hall and about half a dozen cottages. These and the fields around are one of the arcadian parts of the forest. The buildings are perched on a short but quite steep-sided hill if you approach from the south, and from this side they seem a little like a miniature version of a hill village in Italy or Spain. To the south of the churchyard a field drops down to the River Ribble, which is quite wide here on its way to Preston and the sea. About two miles beyond the river, and running parallel to it, the long high ridge of Pendle Hill takes up much of the view, quite bare at all levels and a little forbidding even on a sunny day.

In this impression one is perhaps subconsciously influenced by the many grim stories about this well-known Lancashire 'witch country'. This is the wild, spectacular side of the forest. All of this makes Great Mitton church one of the most beautifully sited churches in England, not just the northwest.

The finest view of the church is the distant one as you approach from the other side of the river to the south. The only other building visible from this point is the tall outline of Great Mitton Hall first built in the fourteenth century but greatly extended in the seventeenth. Closer up the church can be dated to the late thirteenth century by the tracery of its windows. It is a rather plain building consisting of a chancel, aisleless nave and a west tower. It is built of random buff sandstone although the chancel is rendered. On the south side of the churchyard is a very rare fourteenth-

century cross-head. It shows Christ on the cross with the Virgin Mary and St John alongside. The figures are carved with some feeling, although much weathered, with excellent canopies above. These churchyard crosses would have been seen in every churchyard before the Reformation but were ruthlessly destroyed thereafter. This one was found in 1801 buried near by. It may have been deliberately concealed in a county where recusancy, or loyalty to 'the old faith' was widespread (pages 71, 87, 96, 116). The shafthead to which the cross is now attached is modern. The church entrance is on the north side of the nave, from where it can be seen that a much later, Perpendicular Gothic chapel has been added to the chancel on this side. It has its own small west entrance with a coat of arms above it. That may be enough to give experienced church explorers a clue as to its purpose.

The interior is as simple as the exterior but a church has a character quite separate from its architecture as such. Great Mitton church has a 'lived in' atmosphere that tells of a reasonably well-attended church with a

LEFT A rare fourteenth-century cross-head in the churchyard. Much weathered, it shows Christ on the cross with the Virgin Mary (left) and St John the Evangelist with canopies above the figures.

LEFT BELOW The fourteenth-century effigy of a knight.

BELOW Alabaster effigies of Sir Richard Shireburne, who died on 1597, and his wife. Their children and coats of arms are carved on the sieds of the tomb chest.

congregation that takes a pride in it. There are a number of interesting furnishings in the nave. The earliest is the fifteenth-century screen separating it from the chancel. It was brought here from Whalley Abbey at the time of the Dissolution. The doors have a fine carving of the Annunciation. There is an Elizabethan font cover and a pulpit of *c*.1700.

However, the most interesting things at Great Mitton are in the chapel that was referred to above. From inside it is entered through the arcade separating it from the chancel. The huge windows that fill almost the whole of the east and north walls are clearly Perpendicular Gothic and the clear glass floods the chapel with light. The chapel was built in 1594 by Sir Richard Shireburne, whose family had lived at Stonyhurst Hall about four miles away for over 200 years. Two years earlier Sir Richard had started a complete rebuilding of the ancestral home in the grandest Elizabethan manner and the new chapel was to be a family mausoleum. For his own burial he was only just in time for he died in 1597. Over the next 120 years the chapel was filled with fine monuments by the leading sculptors of the times. The collection provides excellent examples of changing funerary sculptural styles, fashion in dresses and to some extent attitudes to life. The oldest monument predates the chapel, a sandstone effigy of a fourteenth-century knight without any inscription to identify it but presumably a Shireburne. After that comes the monument to the Sir Richard Shireburne mentioned above and his wife. Their alabaster effigies lie on a tomb chest on the sides of which are carved figures of their children and coats of arms. Although post-medieval by nearly a century this is still in the medieval tradition. Sir Richard Shireburne Junior, son of the foregoing and his wife face each other across a prayer desk on a hanging wall monument. This was a type widespread in the decades before and after 1600. There are charming vignettes of their children beneath them. The one in a cot indicates the child died during or shortly after birth, a common occurrence at the time. Usually daughters were shown below or behind the mother and sons below or behind the father but here to balance the composition one daughter has been transferred to the other side. Along

ABOVE RIGHT A prayer desk monument to Sir Richard Shireburne and his wife is typical of late-Elizabethan and Jacobean memorials.

RIGHT White marble monument to Sir Richard Shireburne who died in 1657 and his wife Isabel. The pose is as though they were in life. Notice the platform shoes with square toecaps.

the north wall of the chapel is an impressive line of strikingly similar monuments in white marble. We have clearly moved on several generations. The use of imported marbles was rare in the Middle Ages and although the Shireburnes are still lying down on beds or couches their attitudes are less devout, more secular, their hands no longer joined in prayer. Although these monuments represent deaths over a period of some thirty years they were all commissioned together by Isabel Shireburne in 1690 from the noted sculptor William Stanton. Their common origin is evident in the similarity of the poses and treatment of dress – the men, for instance all lie with their knees crossed high and all have remarkably modern looking platform shoes with square toes. The one shown here is that of Richard Shireburne who died in 1657 and his wife Isabel mentioned above. The latest monument in the chapel is also the most moving. It is again by William Stanton and fills most of the west wall. It is for Richard Francis Shireburne, who died in 1702 aged nine years. The little boy is shown life size contemplating a skull and bones at his feet as though he were in a graveyard. Behind him there is a reredos with a pediment below which cherubs flutter.

When young Richard Francis died his father had no heir and the house and estate at Stonyhurst passed by marriage to the Weld family another equally old recusant family. In 1794 Thomas Weld gave Stonyhurst to the Society of Jesus (Jesuit order). Over the next 200 years they built up a nationally famous Catholic public school. The house is an impressive building in beautiful grounds. The original house of 1592 was considerably added to by later Shireburnes, and the school has made extensions in sympathy with the original. It is a story not uncommon all over England: an ancient family gone from a great ancestral house, remembered only by their monuments in the parish church.

ACCESS

The church is often open at weekends. Stonyhurst Hall (now Stonyhurst College) is open during the school holidays in July–August when there is access to the grounds and there are guided tours of the old house and the school. Note: Like Slaidburn Great Mitton was until recently in West Yorkshire and it will be found listed there in many architectural gazeteers such as Pevsner and Betjeman.

LEFT, ABOVE The life-size monument to Richard Francis Shireburne who died in 1702 aged nine years. Angels flutter above as he gazes down on a skull and bones.

LEFT The entrance front to Stonyhurst Hall built in 1592. It was the ancestral home of the Shireburnes whose monuments are in Great Mitton church. Since 1800 it has been a Catholic public school.

ST MARY, WHALLEY, LANCASHIRE

A CHURCH AT THE WALLS OF AN ABBEY

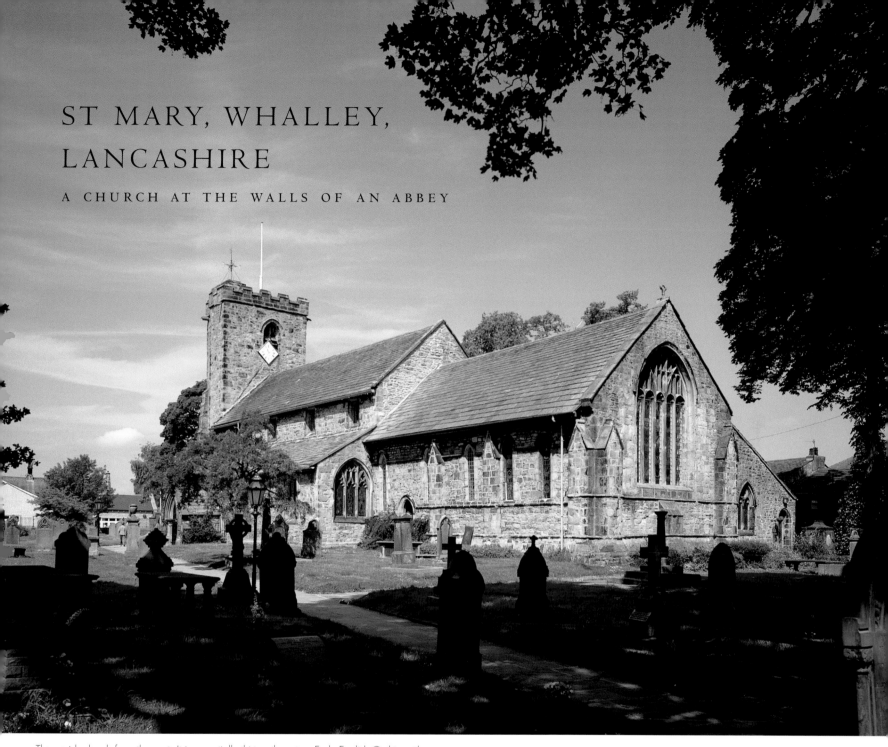

The parish church from the east. It is essentially thirteenth-century Early English Gothic with some later additions.

The small town of Whalley is only a few minutes drive from Great Mitton (pages 55–8). In our journey south through Lancashire we have now crossed the River Ribble and we are approaching that hybrid or transitional region between the county's rural north and industrial south described in the Introduction. Nonetheless Whalley is essentially a country town. From its main street, fields and wooded hills are visible in the near distance. However, like any town today, it is clogged with traffic and it cannot be said to have any special architectural character or prettiness when taken as a whole. The exception to the noise and the lack of character is a secluded enclave at the edge of the town bordered by the River Calder, reached by turning off the busy main street into the narrow Church Lane. Down here there is a wealth of Christian architecture, art and history spanning 1,300 years. Moreover, the sequence in which events developed here is unusual.

Two Saxon crosses in the parish churchyard. One (left) has no Christian symbolism carved on it, the other (right) has a single sacred figure in the centre.

In Church Lane the parish church and a large churchyard are on one side and a long row of attractive stone cottages is on the other. The rest of the buildings we are here to visit lie a little further beyond. By far the earliest things in this historic corner of Whalley are three stone crosses in the churchyard, which are clearly pre-Conquest. Although they were carved at some time in the Saxon period the literature is noncommital as to their dates. They may be much later than the Bewcastle Cross (pages 16–19) but in their crudeness they owe nothing to the culture of the people who created that fine work of art. One of them has no religious iconography at all, the other has a single much-weathered figure of Christ or one of the saints. There is a local tradition, without any evidence to support it, that St Paulinus, who came to England with St Augustine in AD 597 and became the first Bishop of York, visited Whalley, which was part of his diocese, and that the crosses originated in a mission station that he founded here.

However, the church that now stands adjacent to the crosses has no visible traces of Saxon work. In fact there is only slight evidence of a Norman church in the south doorway. The church as it is today is essentially thirteenth-century Early English Gothic. It is a long building because the chancel is almost the same length as the nave. The buff-coloured local Carboniferous sandstone is slightly blackened by centuries of soot deposits. The church was given some Perpendicular Gothic windows and a west tower in the fifteenth century.

The nave has a noble and lofty Early English arcade separating it from the aisles. The church has numerous interesting fittings and furnishings. The most outstanding are the choir stalls, seats and canopies, taken from the

RIGHT Eighteenth- and early-nineteenth-century monuments cover the chancel walls.

The canopies over two of the stalls taken from the adjacent abbey at the Reformation.

The eighteenth-century organ case in the west gallery.

adjacent abbey at the time of the Dissolution (see below). They can be dated to the time of an abbot who reigned from 1418–34. The seats and misericords have been described by Pevsner as 'one of the most rewarding sets in the country'. The misericords, or undersides of the tip-up seats, have carvings typical of their kind in which the medieval carvers had great fun with a wide variety of subjects. Some are religious, e.g. St George fighting the dragon. Most are secular and include delightful vignettes of everyday life, e.g. a man with pigs chasing Reynard the fox who has made off with a goose. Each seat has its own canopy.

There are many monuments spanning 400 years. On a wall in the nave there is a tiny brass to Ralph Caterall (d.1515) and his wife, who kneel facing each other. Their nine sons kneel behind their father and their eleven daughters kneel behind their mother. The chancel walls are covered with eighteenth- and early-nineteenth-century white marble monuments,

some of them very elegantly done. There is a splendid organ case of 1729 in the west gallery. It was brought here from Lancaster priory church (pages 44–7).

The inner gatehouse to Whalley Abbey is just a hundred yards from the church. When an abbey and a parish church occur together in a town there is usually the presumption that the abbey came first, a town developed around it and the parish church followed from that. The sequence of events at Whalley is quite different. As we have seen the parish church was built in the Norman period on a site that had already been in sacred use for some hundreds of years. That first church was rebuilt in the early thirteenth century. The monks did not arrive in Whalley for nearly a hundred years after that. Cistercian monks, whose rule was a stricter and more austere version of that of the Benedictines, had settled at Standlaw, far away on the Wirral peninsula in Cheshire, in c.1170. In the early thirteenth century,

LEFT Two of the fifteenth-century misericords, part of the choir stalls taken from the adjacent abbey at the Dissolution. St George fights the dragon. A man with pigs chases a fox making off with a goose.

LEFT BELOW The memorial brass to Robert Caterall who died in 1515. He kneels facing his wife. Their nine sons kneel behind him and their eleven daughters behind their mother.

because of family connections between their patron the Constable of Chester and a Lancashire family, they came into 'possession' of Blackburn and Rochdale parish churches, i.e. they acquired the right to appoint the rector and claim the major tithes. Later, in 1283, they came into possession of Whalley parish church. During their time at Standlaw the monks suffered from a number of natural disasters. The abbey was situated at the junction of the Rivers Mersey and Goyt and at times flooded to depths of up to five feet (a story that sounds all too modern to someone writing in mid-2007). Gales and fire caused more destruction. The monks petitioned the pope, the king and the appropriate bishops to move to Whalley. There was a succession of complications and it was not until 1319 that the first small vanguard of monks arrived in Whalley, where they lived at first in the rectory. Building work started within a year. Its detailed history cannot concern us here but it proceeded only very slowly. The first mass was not celebrated in the church until 1380. Parts of the domestic quarters were not completed until 1440. Towards the end of the Middle Ages the Cistercians had departed considerably from their original austere way of life. As late as 1510 John Paslew, the last abbot, was enlarging the abbot's lodgings. It follows from this brief building history that the architecture started in the Decorated style and finished in the Perpendicular. The stone is the same as in the parish church, a gritty buff sandstone similarly blackened with age. Paslew may have had a lifestyle not intended by the founders of the Cistercian order in 1100, but at the Dissolution Henry VIII's agents could prove no allegations of immorality, their usual ploy to suppress a religious house. Paslew ended his life bravely. He refused either to take the oath of royal supremacy acknowledging the king as head of the Church of England or to surrender his abbey, and he was hanged for high treason at Lancaster Castle (pages 44–7) on 9 March 1539.

After the Dissolution the property was sold to Richard Assheton, a member of the family who had rebuilt Middleton church shortly before (pages 72–7). He converted the already large abbot's lodgings into an even larger family mansion and pulled down the abbey church and some of the cloister buildings. Others decayed gradually with time. The property passed through several other hands until happily it was bought for the diocese of Manchester in 1923. Since then it has passed to the newer diocese of Blackburn, who use the abbot's lodging-turned-mansion as a conference centre. It is an idyllically peaceful place for that purpose, the house now surrounded by lawns where the church and cloister once stood with the River Calder flowing alongside.

Apart from the mansion there are still some significant survivals. The inner gateway into the abbey precincts is entirely intact but more moving is the outer gateway giving into the abbey estate about a quarter of a mile away on a quiet lane at the edge of the town. In the cloister the entrance to the chapter house survives with fine carvings as does the abbot's kitchen and its drain. The remains of the reredorter (lavatory block) and its drainage system over the river are still a monumental piece of engineering.

The church, therefore, has been in possession of these acres at Whalley and active within them for about 1,300 years: a Saxon missionary site, an early-medieval parish church and a late-medieval abbey, followed by a return of the whole area to ecclesiastical use in the twentieth century.

ACCESS

The parish church is open most afternoons. The abbey grounds are open every day (entrance fee). There is a café, visitor centre and shop.

LEFT The outer gatehouse into the abbey estate is on a quiet lane at the edge of the town.

ABOVE RIGHT The abbot's kitchen and its drain.

RIGHT The entrance to the chapter house from the cloister. Note the ornate carvings.

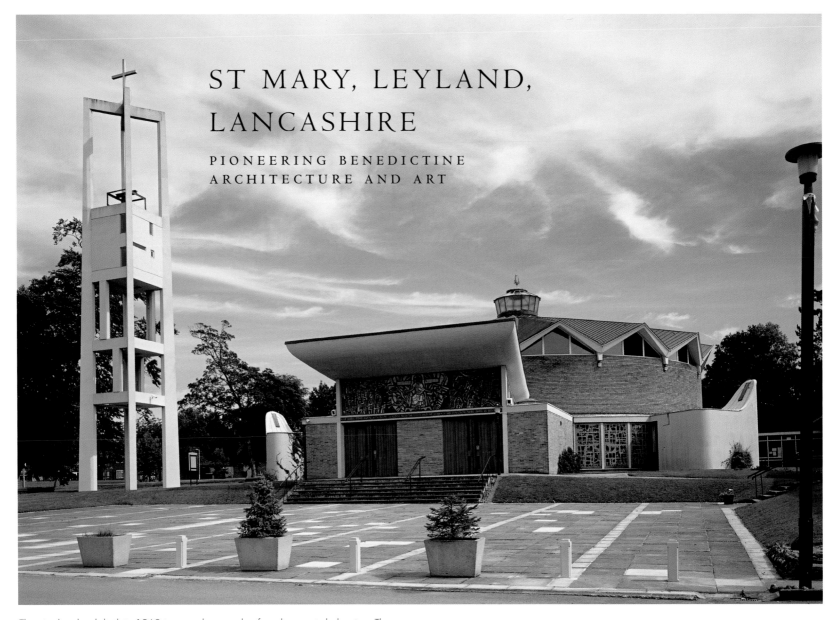

ST MARY, LEYLAND, LANCASHIRE

PIONEERING BENEDICTINE ARCHITECTURE AND ART

The circular church built in 1962 is an early example of modern central planning. The detached campanile has an open concrete frame.

Leyland is a town about five miles south of Preston. Open countryside is only a few minutes in a car from its centre but it has the character of a suburb rather than a country town. Modern estate houses far outnumber anything earlier. The Roman Catholic parish of Leyland has been served by Benedictine monks of Ampleforth Abbey in North Yorkshire for several generations. When in the 1950s it became necessary to replace an older church, priests of the Benedictine order could call upon 1,500 years experience of traditional and innovative church building throughout Europe. At that time they were also in the forefront of liturgical reform aimed at the needs of modern congregations, so a safe traditionalism was probably never an option for the new Leyland church. The then parish priest travelled Europe to see what was being created there by architects who were more innovative than their contempories in Britain. He came back with ideas for a 'centrally planned' church in which the high altar would be at the middle. That plan is commonplace now but then it was startling and even an irreverent idea to worshippers who were used to 'longnitudinally planned' churches in which the altar was set apart at one end and the congregation faced it in front. The new church was built in 1962–4 to the design of Weightman and Bullen, architects to the Catholic archdiocese of Liverpool, and it was 'one of their best churches', according to Pevsner. A little earlier,

A general view of the interior with the high altar at the centre, similar to Liverpool Catholic Cathedral (pages 116–23).

in 1960 Frederick Gibberd had won the competition to design the archdiocese's new cathedral for which a central plan had been prescribed by the archbishop (pages 116–23). There are marked similarities in plan and in detail between the cathedral and the Leyland church.

St Mary is a round church of brick and concrete. A radially folded roof joins the upper walls in zig-zag gables. There is a detached open framework campanile of concrete posts, taller than the church. The building is approached by broad steps to a projecting vestibule with a canopy, below which there is a mosaic of the Last Judgement. It is rather like medieval 'doom paintings' above chancel arches, which showed the saved and the damned on either side of the triumphant figure of Christ.

The vestibule leads into a wide ambulatory passage that encircles the whole interior. It has its own roof lower than the body of the church from which it is separated by a ring of forked concrete pillars. From the ambulatory the floor of the church slopes down slightly to the centre and the altar so that from all the circular benches there is a good view of the latter. The overall effect is that of a covered arena.

The church is lit by clear glass in the ring of gables above the side walls and by a small lantern tower above the altar. The glass that dominates the whole interior, however, is the remarkable set of thirty-six abstract stained-

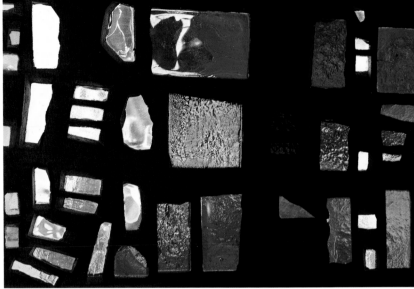

A panel detail. Irregularly shaped pieces of thick glass are each set separately in concrete.

TOP The ambulatory all around the church has thirty-six abstract stained-glass windows as the most striking feature of the interior.

ABOVE Two of the panels show how predominantly blue colours were used throughout.

glass windows that form the outer wall of the ambulatory in a single unified scheme. They were designed by Patrick Reyntiens, who did the principal glass, also abstract, at Liverpool Catholic Cathedral. Each window is about ten feet by six feet set between concrete pillars, 'very beautiful in colours and shapes' (Pevsner). Each of the small, thick irregularly shaped pieces that together form a window is set into concrete. It is a popular form of modern glazing known as dalles de verre (literally 'paving stones of glass'). Dark blue colours predominate with some greens and violets. An isolated bright red appears in a few windows.

For services involving smaller congregations and for individual prayer and meditation there are a number of attractively designed side-chapels.

The artwork throughout the church is, as would be expected, of a much higher quality than in Catholic churches elsewhere of the early twentieth century. The Liverpool sculptor Arthur Dooley created a set of bronze Stations of the Cross, which are arranged on the pillars around the ambulatory. Other distinguished artists were commissioned to make statues in wood and metal, tapestries and lettering.

Many parish churches, Roman Catholic, Anglican and Free Church have since followed in the architectural footsteps of Leyland, their architects developing a large number of variations on the central plan which clearly satisfies the modern desire for services involving a closer relationship between ministers and people, between altar and pew.

ACCESS

There are generally two or more services each day.

ST WILFRID, STANDISH, GREATER MANCHESTER

A REMARKABLE MIXTURE OF ARCHITECTURAL TRADITION AND INNOVATION

Standish is a town about four miles north of Wigan, which means that it was once at the heart of the Lancashire coalmining industry. That industry is now mainly part of history and its disappearance has changed the face of many northern towns physically and socially. Physically it has removed many scars: the air and the buildings are cleaner, the tall ugly machinery at the pitheads that once dominated the skylines has gone and slag heaps and the like have been levelled and grassed over. However, social scars have been created, as many men were made redundant. Despite the fact that Standish is an industrial town one can be out on the high Lancashire moors to the north, west and east within minutes in a car.

Pevsner described Standish church as 'one of the most interesting churches in Lancashire'. As an architectural historian he was apt to make these judgements on the basis of historical innovation or peculiarity as much as on appearance. St Wilfrid is a large church in a large churchyard at the centre of the town. It is stylistically uniform, i.e. Perpendicular Gothic throughout, recognisable by the huge windows, their tracery and the battlements above them. Whatever earlier churches were here we know the exact dates of the final rebuilding. In 1544 the church was 'in grete ruyne' and the contract for rebuilding it in 1582–4 still exists. It is therefore the very latest Perpendicular in a time when church building had virtually ceased as a result of the turmoil of the Reformation. At that time mens' hands were more likely to

East view of the church, a good example of an entirely Perpendicular Gothic building with characteristically large windows and battlements above. It was built at an unusual time 1582–4, just after the Reformation.

Cartouche to Edward Chisnall, a Royalist soldier killed in the English Civil War in 1653. It is typically Baroque in its exuberant use of colour and variety of motifs, heraldry, drapes, angels, swords and trumpets.

One of several funeral hatchments in the church. They were placed in parish churches following the death of a prominent person. The husband's arms are on the left (as viewed) and his wife's on the right. The white background of hers tells that she survived him.

have been turning to destruction rather than creation of ecclesiastical buildings. The church has a tall west spire renewed in the nineteenth century and there are also two prominent turrets at the meeting of the nave and chancel. Standish is a return to our journey down the west side of the Pennines so yet again we see here the blackened gritty sandstone of the region in the church.

Architecture apart, the church has a warm, welcoming, much-used feeling inside. There are carpets in all the aisles and although the lower windows have much dark glass the upper clerestory windows have clear glass so the church is pleasantly bright. If the architecture of the exterior maintained the long Perpendicular tradition of the later Middle Ages, that of the interior moved to a revolutionary innovation. The five-bay nave arcade separating it from the aisles has pointed Gothic arches as we would expect but the great surprise is that the columns that support them are no longer Gothic but Roman 'Tuscan' columns of the Italian Renaissance. They are cylindrical on high pedestals with square classical abaci above at the junctions with the arches. Strictly speaking, in classical architecture there should be either a horizontal architrave or a set of round-headed arches above the abaci. It is as though the designer lost his innovative nerve when it came to the arches and reverted to the familiar and safe Gothic. The year 1584 is early for the use of major Renaissance elements in church architecture in England. Even in London, the usual centre of innovation, such forms were being used only after 1600. Their use in the provincial north before that is remarkable, particularly when taken in conjunction with a resolutely traditionally Gothic exterior. There is another architectural curiosity in the church. In the rebuilding of 1582, although the Protestant Reformation was fully complete and secure in Elizabethan England, provision was clearly made for a rood screen and loft above it, definitely 'Catholic' features, and stairs leading to the latter are within the piers of the chancel arch. The two turrets outside, remarked upon previously, were designed to be above them. It must be assumed that the rector and churchwardens had 'popish' leanings and were optimistic that Protestantism in England was to be a short-lived phenomenon (or aberration) only, with an eventual return to Catholicism. This idea fits with the fact mentioned in a number of places that Lancashire was a strongly recusant county from the start.

The church has monuments from the fourteenth to the nineteenth century. The cartouche to Edward Chisnall on the south chancel arch faces down the church and gives a bright splash of colour to the nave. He was a Royalist soldier killed in the English Civil War in 1653, aged thirty-five. With its exuberant variety of motifs, heraldry, cherubs, drapes, swords and trumpets it is more typical of the Baroque art of a generation later. The pulpit is a fine piece of 1616 but still Elizabethan in style. There are several funeral hatchments hanging on the walls of the church. These will be seen in many pre-Victorian churches where the parish was the home to an aristocratic or otherwise prominent family, in this case the Standish family. When the head of the family or his wife died the coats of arms of both his and her families were painted on a diamond shaped board or canvas and displayed outside the family seat for some months before being deposited in the parish church. In both the hatchments seen in the photographs, the left half (as seen by the viewer but called the dexter or right side in heraldry) has a black background and the other half a white background. The former has the arms of the husband and shows that he died first, to be survived by his wife. In the opposite event the background colours would be reversed. A single man deceased would have a hatchment filled with a single coat of arms with a black background. Hatchments were rarely made after the accession of Queen Victoria. High quality furnishings continued to be installed in Standish church in the twentieth century. The large chancel east window has richly glowing glass of 1963 by the noted glass artist Harry Stammers of York. The chancel was reordered to suit the modern litury by George Pace at about the same time, done in an exemplary way.

This apparently unremarkable section of the nave arcade of 1584 is in fact a historical landmark architecturally. The designer started with classical Renaissance columns on high pedestals below and with classical abaci above but then reverted to typically pointed Gothic arches. Classical features are rare in pre-1600 church architecture.

ACCESS

The church is open most days. Guidebooks are on sale.

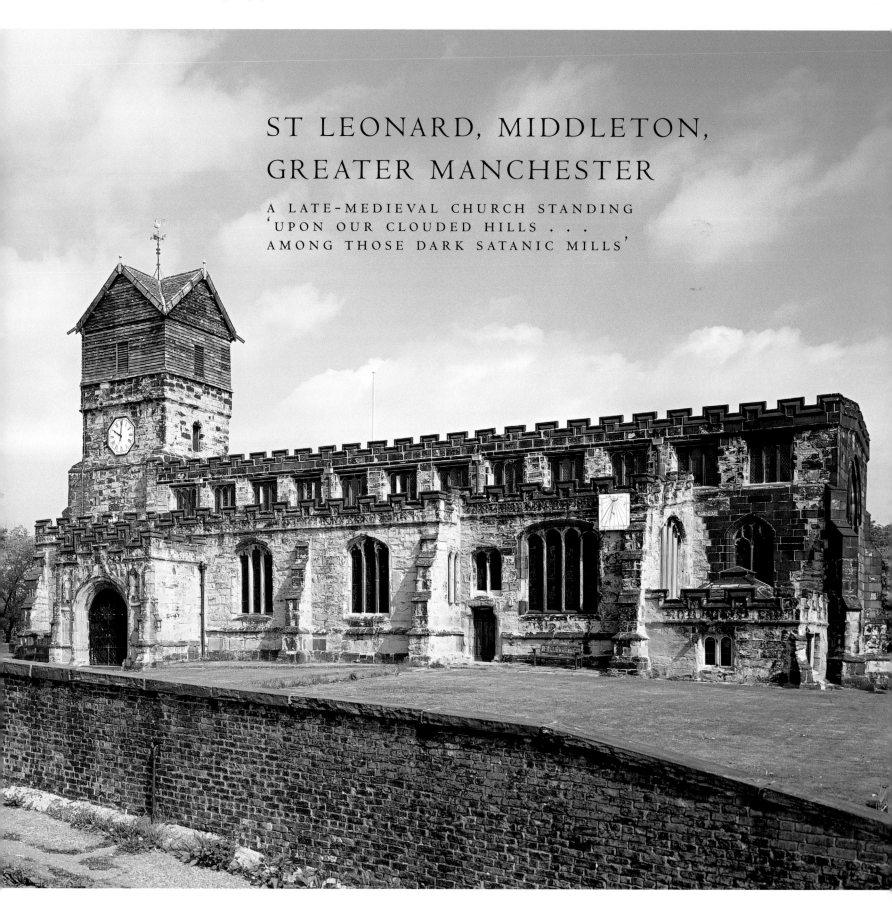

ST LEONARD, MIDDLETON, GREATER MANCHESTER

A LATE-MEDIEVAL CHURCH STANDING
'UPON OUR CLOUDED HILLS . . .
AMONG THOSE DARK SATANIC MILLS'

LEFT Middleton church from the south. The visible features are all fifteenth- and sixteenth-century but the interior has twelfth-century Norman work.

BELOW The splendid view eastwards towards the Pennine hills in the distance. In the foreground the nineteenth-century mills and their chimneys seen in the bright sunlight of the twenty-first century do not seem as 'satanic' as William Blake described them.

In the early Middle Ages Middleton was a village, which later grew to a township, seven miles northeast of Manchester. Since the early twentieth century progressive expansion of the city has joined the two together so that those driving through it today on the main road between Manchester and Rochdale might get the impression that Middleton is like any characterless outer suburb of a northern city. However, any familiarity with the town soon dispels that impression. To its north, west and east the built landscape gives way to fields but what distinguishes Middleton from an ordinary suburb is that it lies in the western foothills of the Pennines. The centre of the town is on lower ground and the streets radiating from it climb quite steeply. From many street corners and in between houses there are distant views to the Pennines. There are a small number of medieval buildings, one of which we have come here to see, but the main impression is of the mid- and late nineteenth century with row upon row of terraced houses built of the local millstone grit sandstone or brick. They are of the two-up-two-down type, many of them letting directly on to the streets in a way made familiar to the nation from television's *Coronation Street*, set in neighbouring Salford. On the growing

edges of the town there are, of course, many more modern houses. In the nineteenth century the cotton industry came to much of the area, Middleton included, creating vast mills with tall chimneys. The cotton has gone now and the mills are converted to engineering works, showrooms, cash-and-carry stores and the like.

The parish church of St Leonard is boldly and prominently sited on top of a steep hill about 200 yards north of the town centre. From the spacious hilltop churchyard crammed with blackened sandstone monuments both grandiose and humble, there are views over the town for about six miles to Manchester in the south and to Oldham and the Pennines in the east. The mills and their chimneys are visible in the foreground and in the middle distance. It is a scene that the Salford painter L.S. Lowry (1887–1976) would have appreciated and which would have rung a chord with William Blake, author of the well-known mystical poem-hymn 'Jerusalem'.

The church is built of coarse-grained Pennine sandstone. Like the gravestones its gritty surface has caught the smoke of thousands of domestic and industrial chimneys over the last 200 years but a considerable flaking away of the stone has revealed an attractive golden colour beneath in many places. The church consists of an aisled nave, chancel and west tower. The tower has a distinctive weather-boarded top stage with four gables. Externally the church appears all Perpendicular Gothic and we know that a Middleton man, Cardinal Thomas Langley (c.1370–1427), Bishop of Durham, Keeper of the Privy Seal and Chancellor to Henry IV, paid for and himself consecrated a substantially new building in 1412. In the following century the local lord of the

LEFT The Norman arch into the west tower has typical zig-zag decoration of the time but its original round arch was reset to a Gothic point at some later time.

RIGHT The late-seventeenth-century 'horse box' pew of the local Hopwood family.

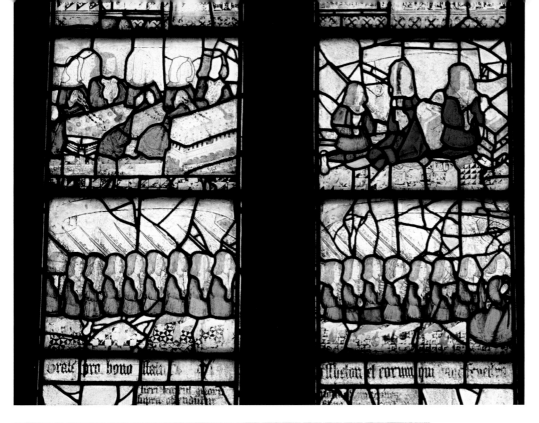

manor, Richard Assheton, remodelled the church again in 1524, leaving only the tower and sumptuous south porch of Langley's church.

However, when we enter the church we can immediately see its much earlier origins. The arch from the nave into the west tower is Norman with the chevron (zig-zag) decoration, which was ubiquitous throughout much of the twelfth century. In a later resetting the originally round arch was made pointed in the Gothic manner. The rest of the interior is mainly of Assheton's rebuilding.

The most interesting feature from the late Middle Ages is a chancel window of c.1530 commemorating the battle of Flodden in 1513 in which the forces of Henry VIII defeated those of James IV of Scotland in the north of England. Richard Assheton took sixteen Middleton archers and a chaplain to the battle. The window shows the Assheton family in the upper half and below, chaplain Henricus Tayler in front of the archers. They, like the family above, are all shown kneeling. The archers all carry their longbows with their individual names inscribed below the figures. This must be one of the earliest 'war memorial' windows in England. Richard Assheton was knighted for his services to the King and his rebuilding of the parish church may have been connected with the victory and his knighthood.

The rood screen is original in the dado (lower solid part). This also is of the time of Sir Richard or a little later and, with its square panels of heraldic arms, it is an early indicator of the coming Renaissance in England when classical forms replaced Gothic. There are several early-sixteenth-century Assheton brasses in the chancel floor, including one for an Assheton rector. In the south aisle is a large family pew of the Hopwood family from nearby Hopwood Hall. These structures of the late seventeenth century are aptly called 'horse box' pews, solid below with twisted balusters above. There are some handsome early-twentieth-century windows by Christopher Whall, a follower of the pre-Raphaelites (pages 24–32).

Visitors to Middleton parish church come away with an unusual mixture of impressions in which images of the early and late Middle Ages mingle with those of a recent but now rapidly disappearing northern industrial past.

ACCESS

The church is open some afternoons each week from Easter until autumn.

LEFT Gem-like glass of 1911 by Christopher Whall, a follower of the Pre-Raphaelites (pages 24–32). The virtue of Love is represented by Christ (centre) and those of Faith and Hope by female allegorical figures.

TOP Glass of c.1530 commemorating the Battle of Flodden in 1513 to which Richard Assheton, the lord of the manor, took sixteen Middleton archers and a chaplain. The archers below in blue carry their longbows (just visible). The chaplain, Henricus Tayler, kneels in front of them (right).

ABOVE The lower part of the rood screen of c.1530 shows something of the spirit of the coming Renaissance in England.

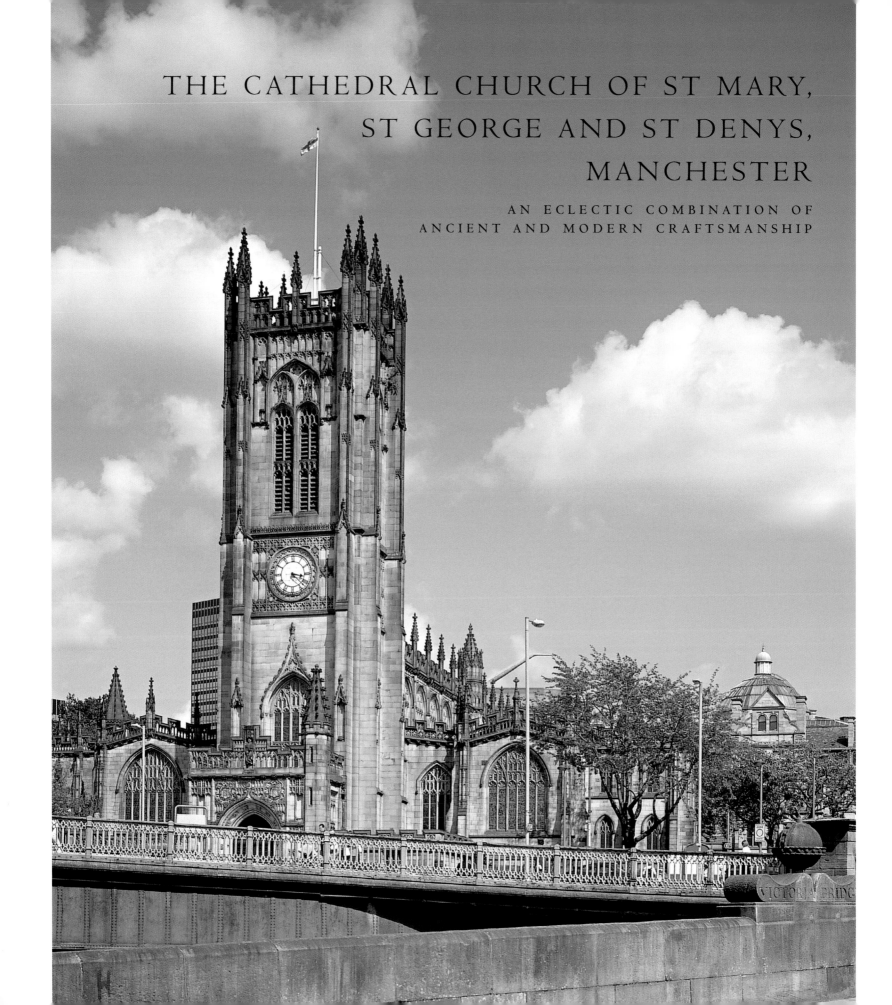

THE CATHEDRAL CHURCH OF ST MARY, ST GEORGE AND ST DENYS, MANCHESTER

AN ECLECTIC COMBINATION OF ANCIENT AND MODERN CRAFTSMANSHIP

The Anglican diocese of Manchester was created in 1847 when it was carved out of the diocese of Chester. This was thirty-three years before its arch-rival Liverpool (pages 98–104). Liverpool at first used a city-centre parish church as a cathedral before deciding soon afterwards to build anew on a grand scale. Manchester also chose a large city-centre parish church — and stayed with it. The result is a modern cathedral in an ancient church. It is at the centre of the city in the commonly perceived sense, surrounded by its principal shopping and business areas at the north end of Deansgate, a straight mile-long street that cuts through the heart of the city. Paradoxically it is also at the edge of the city because the west end of the cathedral is only a few yards from the River Irwell, which is the boundary between the cities of Manchester and Salford. This has always been a purely administrative boundary; Manchester and Salford merge seamlessly into one another architecturally and socially. Furthermore the historic centre of Salford is situated on and around the river bank only half a mile upstream where St Philip's church (page 91) was built in what was then a quiet residential area of Georgian houses.

There was a church on or close to the site of the present cathedral from a very early time. On display inside is a stone with a carving of an angel that is probably late Saxon. An early medieval Gothic church followed. In 1421 Thomas de la Warre was Lord of the Manor of Manchester, then a small town, and he was also a priest. He obtained a licence from Henry V to found a 'collegiate' church on the same site. The collegiate church was to have a warden, eight fellows (priests), four lay clerks and six boy choristers. The college was to be a place of communal prayer with the daily offices of the Church, study and teaching. It was also to be a place of pastoral care for the huge sixty-square-mile parish of Manchester whose spiritual condition was a concern to de la Warre. The church was also to have a number of chantry chapels where the priests would say masses each day for Henry V, de la Warre and the Bishop of Lichfield (in whose diocese Manchester then was; the diocese of Chester was only created by Henry VIII at the Reformation). It was dedicated to St Mary, St George and St Denys (the latter because Henry V had married a daughter of the French king). Residential accommodation was built to the north of the church for the establishment and that too still survives (see below). The starting of building of the new church in 1421 meant that it was in the Perpendicular Gothic style. Building, re-building and extensions in the form of chapels continued for over a hundred years under successive wardens but only experts can analyse the exact chronology from contemporary documents. The church

OPPOSITE The cathedral from the southwest. It was built in Perpendicular Gothic style in 1421–1520, originally as a collegiate parish church. The parapet in the foreground is on a bridge over the River Irwell.

ABOVE The sixteenth-century screen separating the nave from the choir beyond.

underwent several major restorations in the nineteenth century before and after its elevation to a cathedral. Unlike most Victorian restorations the work enhanced the church. The west tower was heightened and decorated with battlements and pinnacles. Grand porches were added on the west, south and north sides. Most of the external stonework was refaced during these operations using buff sandstone from Lancashire and Derbyshire quarries, so the building looks less old than it is. The cathedral does not have the spacious grounds of its medieval counterparts in other dioceses. At the east and west ends it abuts directly on to the street pavements. On the north and south sides there are small lawns just large enough to give the building breathing space.

The interior is a surprise in several ways. Firstly, when standing at the centre of the back of the cathedral one is struck by the great width; it is almost as wide as it is long. The nave has the usual aisles north and south but then again another set of aisles beyond these so that there are five parallel spaces running from west to east. They are separated by slender piers which minimise the division between them with a feeling of airiness and of space flowing easily from one part to the next. Before the Reformation the outer aisles would not have appeared as such since they were actually a series of side-chapels or chantry chapels adjacent to one another. Their removal after the Reformation created the continuous spaces on either side of the inner aisles that we have today. The second surprise for those conscious of the

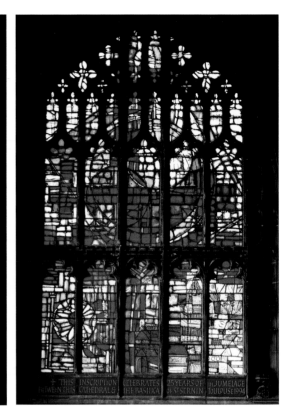

ABOVE Three of the five windows at the west end of the cathedral, inserted in 1972–95 which flood the building with colour. The abstract designs represent 'Creation' (left) 'Revelation' (centre) and St Denys (right), who is one of the church's patrons.

LEFT The sumptuously carved canopies over the early-sixteenth-century choir stalls are among the finest in England.

materials of which a building is made is that the (unrenewed) stone inside is New Red Sandstone from Delamere in Cheshire. The more modern stone flags are a handsome shelly Carboniferous limestone from Derbyshire. Thirdly, as you wander round the building you are struck by the marked contrasts between areas of darkness and of bright colour in the furnishings. The dark is the magnificent old oak woodwork in the choir and elsewhere; the colour is the equally magnificent modern windows at the west and east ends. These dark and colourful things are the most outstanding features of the cathedral.

The chancel and nave are separated by a handsome sixteenth-century screen with open panels and tracery, restored and gilded in the nineteenth century. Within are the most famous things in the cathedral: the choir stalls with a complete set of canopies and misericords. They were installed by the third warden, John Stanley, in *c*.1505–10. The oak is now almost black with ageing. The most intricately carved canopies rise to a height of about twelve feet. Above the first stage of each is another tier and then a cresting with segmental arches on pendants. The full set of misericords has charming scenes from everyday life. Church carpenters often showed a quirky sense of humour when carving misericords, and here they have excelled themselves. There is a rabbit cooking a hunter; a man breaking his wife's cooking pot; a sow playing bagpipes for other pigs and a man being robbed by monkeys.

The colour areas of the cathedral come from the present time. The west end has five large windows corresponding to the nave and the four aisles. From 1972–95 Antony Hollaway designed five rather complex abstract pictures representing the three patrons, the Blessed Virgin Mary, St George and St Denys, 'Creation' and 'Revelation'. The east end of the cathedral was damaged by a landmine on 24 December 1940. It involved extensive restoration work after the end of the war and as part of this another piece of colour, the eye-catching window in the northeast chapel was designed by Margaret Traherne to show the flames of the burning cathedral just as they might have looked on that dreadful Christmas Eve.

There are surprisingly few monuments for a church of this age and size. One of the most interesting is a large brass in the chancel to John Huntingdon, the first warden from 1422–58 who is shown wearing choir dress. Another is the monument to Humphrey Chetham. When the college and chantry chapels were dissolved at the Reformation the extensive domestic quarters a hundred yards north of the church survived because they were bought by the Earl of Derby. Pevsner describes them as 'the best preserved buildings of their type and age in the country'. In the middle of the seventeenth century they were bought by the executors of the will of Humphrey Chetham, a wealthy local businessman who died in 1653. Under the terms of his will a free library and a Bluecoat Charity School were founded in the following year. The original fifteenth-century buildings were preserved in good condition but added to by a number of distinguished nineteenth architects as the school expanded. The charity school continued until after the Second World War when it became Chetham's School Of Music, a nationally and internationally famous centre of training for young musicians. In Chetham's monument a young Bluecoat boy in his frock coat sits at the founder's feet.

As a collegiate and parish church up to the middle of the nineteenth century, this was a building on a grand scale. As a cathedral it is undoubtedly on a small scale but suits the diocese well. What it lacks in size it has gained in the beauty of its eclectic furnishings and its welcoming intimacy.

ACCESS

The cathedral is open every day. There is a visitor centre with café and shop. Chetham School buildings are open to visitors on certain days each year.

ABOVE RIGHT Monument to Humphrey Chetham, who died in 1653. He founded a Bluecoat Charity School in the nearby clergy house of the former collegiate church. A frock-coated pupil of the school sits at his feet. The building is now occupied by a famous music school.

RIGHT Glass of 1966 by Margaret Traherne representing the fire started by incendiary bombs that destroyed the east end of the cathedral on Christmas Eve 1940.

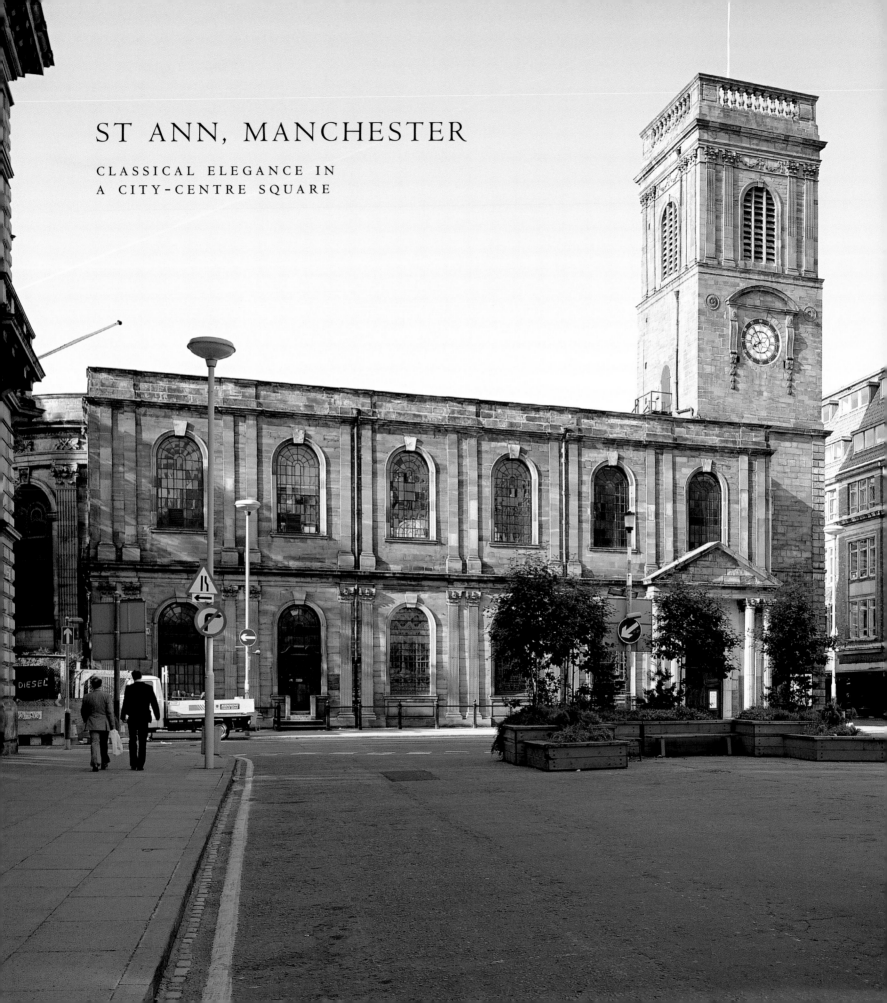

ST ANN, MANCHESTER

CLASSICAL ELEGANCE IN
A CITY-CENTRE SQUARE

St Ann's church is a handsome early-eighteenth-century classical building which now forms the north side of St Ann's Square, a small busy and attractive shopping enclave in the heart of Manchester. The square has gained from the recent exclusion of traffic and by the splash of green provided by the planting of a number of trees. It is only a few hundred yards south of the present cathedral (pages 78–81), although when the church was built the cathedral was only the parish church of a small town that had expanded little since the Middle Ages. The place where the church stands was an open site on the edge of the town where a fair had been held since the fourteenth century.

The church was built in 1709–12, paid for by Lady Anne Bland, daughter of Sir Edward Mosley, lord of the manor of Manchester who lived near by. The creation of the square followed in 1720. Lady Anne's decision to build a new church only 500 yards from a large existing parish church was based on churchmanship and politics. The clergy at the parish church were High Church, Tory and Jacobite. The Mosley family and their circle were Low Church and Whig and the new church was to provide for people of their views. The dedication to St Ann, the mother of the Virgin Mary, was natural for a patron called Anne but perhaps it was also a diplomatic gesture from a Whig to the reigning monarch, Queen Anne, whose position on the throne had resulted from the deposition of the Catholic James II by the 'Glorious Revolution' of 1688.

The church survives externally almost as it was built. Rather less survives of the eighteenth-century square. The west side is partly original, with a row of tall four-storey houses with narrow frontages to the street, ground space in towns being as scarce and expensive in those days as these. The early date of these houses is easily overlooked since the ground floors have been converted to modern shops. The east side now consists of two well-designed late-nineteenth-century banks and part of the enormous and grand former Cotton Exchange built in 1914–21 replacing several earlier versions for a trade that was then at the heart of the city's prosperity. The south side is now largely open to give access to the adjacent streets. The three sides of the church not facing the square are surrounded by a three-sided courtyard-cum-passageway, a quiet, intimate place with shops and old pubs which have pavement dining areas. At the east end of the church a number of mid-eighteenth-century tombs, chests and slabs, have been

The early-eighteenth-century church and square on a Sunday morning before it was crowded with shoppers and visitors.

The pavement tables of a café (right) are close to the east end of the church and the group of tombstones next to it.

assembled together immediately next to the chancel wall, separated from the pavement only by a handrail. Café diners and drinkers only a few feet away have thus a close reminder of their mortality – not something that is common in city centres.

The church consists of a chancel with an apsidal (semi-circular) east end, a nave with north and south aisles and a west tower. The nave has large round-headed windows with pilasters of the Corinthian order between them. There are three handsome doorways at the west end; those on the south and north sides have large pediments supported by four tall columns; the one beneath the tower is simpler. In the Introduction it was suggested that visitors to a church might find it enjoyable and instructive to examine the stone of which it is built. Nowhere in England is this truer than at St Ann's, and here it provides an astonishing sight. The entire wall surface of the church is a veritable patchwork quilt of different coloured stones. They are all ashlar (smoothly cut) work,

The interior has a three-sided gallery for a church that was designed principally as an auditorium for preaching.

which we would expect in a city-centre building, but they come from no less than five different sandstone quarries in the north of England. The most striking of these is a uniquely coloured blue-purple stone from the Collyhurst district of Manchester just a mile away (and another example of a New Red Sandstone not living up to its name). Like many of the same geological formation it is a friable stone (page 14) and repairs have had to be effected at various times. Replacement stones have come from Darley Dale, Derbyshire (greyish yellow); Hollington, Staffordshire (pink); Runcorn, Cheshire (dark red) and Parbold, Lancashire (buff). This mixture is a geologist's paradise, unique and fascinating.

The interior is also substantially as it was built; the changes that have been made have not significantly altered its character. There is a gallery around three sides supported on squat Tuscan columns below and slimmer columns above. The seating in these galleries is steeply raked to provide a clear view of the preacher. In the nave and aisles the former box pews were lowered and their doors removed in the nineteenth century but their effect is still one of smooth

elegance. The preacher has been mentioned because in a 'low' church such as this preaching was regarded as all-important, more so perhaps at that time than the celebration of the Eucharist, a service held quite rarely. The original pulpit survives but not in its original position or its original appearance. As erected it stood between chancel and nave, right at the centre, not to one side as in churches today. This 'Low' or 'Puritan' arrangement gave the pulpit precedence over the altar far behind against the east wall of the chancel. Sight lines to and from the preacher were more important than sight of the altar and for that purpose the pulpit was about ten feet high. It is now to one side of the chancel and only about six feet high – but it has not been cut down. A well was excavated in the floor a little wider than the pulpit, which was then lowered into it – an interesting example of adaptation without mutilation. The small elegant marble font with an octagonal bowl on a baluster stem is the original of 1712. The windows were all originally clear glass since the Puritan church disliked the idea of a 'dim religious light'. Since the nineteenth century coloured glass has been inserted in several of them. The most

LEFT The original marble font of 1712. RIGHT This mid-eighteenth-century window showing the apostles Peter, James and John is a good example of a painted as opposed to a stained glass window.

windows made in 1769 was brought to St Ann's from another Manchester church, now demolished, in 1981. It depicts the apostles Peter, James and John. There are several attractive nineteenth- and twentieth-century stained-glass windows.

St Ann's Square has always been at the centre of a number of fashionable and expensive shopping streets and it remains so today. But Manchester city centre has changed enormously in the last ten years. In 1996 a huge IRA terrorist bomb exploded just 200 yards away, demolishing buildings on a vast scale. The church was shielded from the blast by intervening buildings and so escaped serious damage although many of the windows were blown out. The streets around the square have since seen the arrival of innumerable large buildings in an unmistakably modern twenty-

interesting of these is not stained glass but painted or enamelled glass. The former was the traditional method of giving colour to most medieval glass where coloured metal oxides were added to the molten glass so that the colour was fully part of the material when it solidified. A cartoon of the required picture was drawn on a white table and pieces of the desired coloured glasses were cut to shape using this. Dozens, or even hundreds of these small pieces were assembled using lead strips whose black outlines in a window are an essential part of its character. An entirely different technique is to 'paint' coloured materials mixed with finely ground glass and oil onto a single large piece of glass and then to fire it. The resulting colour is on the surface only. This method was used for small sections of a window, such as faces in the later Middle Ages but it was not until the seventeenth century that whole windows were commonly made in this way. The effect is quite different from medieval glass or the Gothic Revival glass of the nineteenth century. It is a translucent form of a painting on canvas. The most talented English glass painter in the eighteenth century was William Peckitt of York. One of his

first-century style with interesting and novel plans and elevations and lots of glass and metal. There are several shopping malls, hotels, apartments, restaurants and cafés. Attractive small open spaces with fountains and cascades provide places for outdoor dining and drinking (it does not rain continuously in Manchester). As you stand in the square facing the church the most recent addition (2007) in the near distance is the breathtakingly tall forty-seven-storey Beetham Tower, half hotel and half apartments. Several times a year the square itself is filled with stalls for the day, often organised on a themed basis selling continental foods, artwork, etc., so that history has come full circle here.

ACCESS

St Ann's is open all day, every day and it has an especially warm, welcoming atmosphere with somebody always in attendance. Guidebooks can be purchased. Worship takes place daily and there are regular lunchtime and evening concerts.

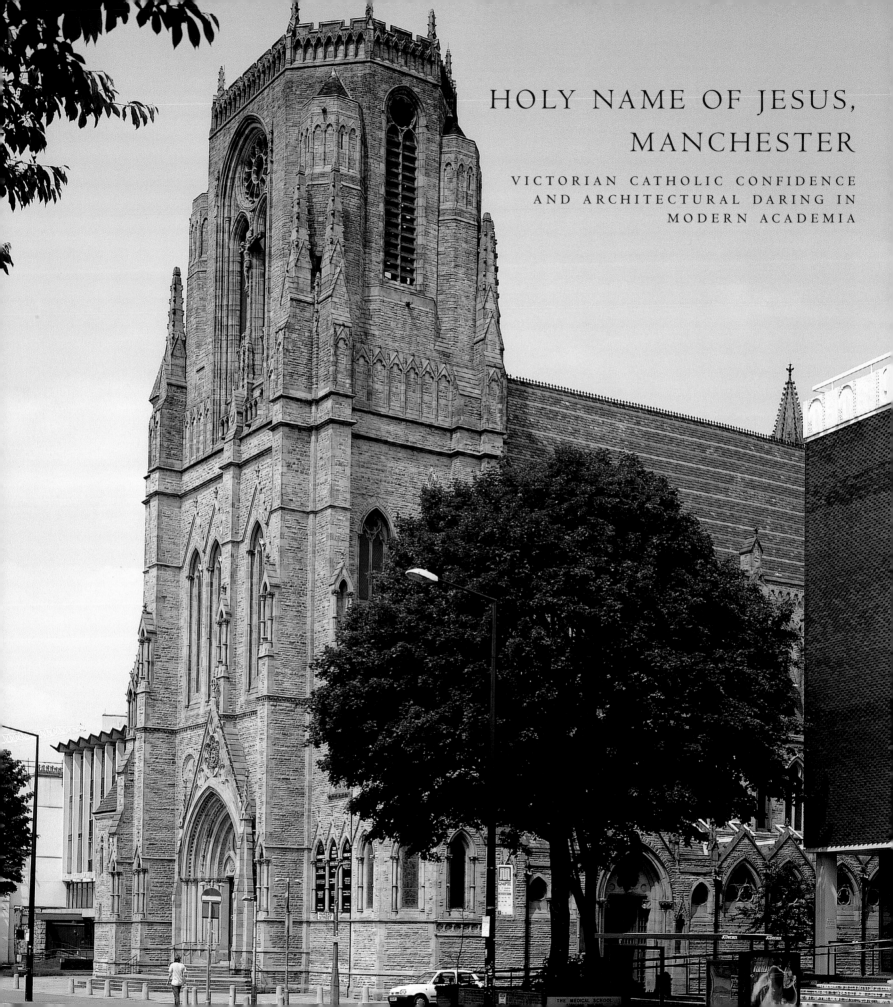

HOLY NAME OF JESUS, MANCHESTER

VICTORIAN CATHOLIC CONFIDENCE AND ARCHITECTURAL DARING IN MODERN ACADEMIA

The rood statues in the tower at the belfry stage.

The prominent pulpit is reminiscent of eighteenth-century structures in Anglican churches, here a symbol of the preaching abilities of the Jesuits.

In the late 1860s the then Roman Catholic Bishop of Salford, of which diocese Manchester forms a part, asked the Society of Jesus (Jesuits) to start a new parish in Chorlton-on-Medlock, a mile south of the city centre. A major religious order like this had access to financial resources not available to a diocese of mainly working-class Catholics. The site chosen for the church was Oxford Road, then a quiet suburb with many Georgian houses but now one of the best-known thoroughfares in the city, particularly to people in academic life. The Jesuits commissioned Joseph Aloysius Hansom (1803–82) to design the church. His name, of course, is best known from the Hansom cab, which he designed. One of his first commissions was to build

The massive tower of the church built in 1869–71 dominates this part of Oxford Road in Manchester's university quarter.

Birmingham Town Hall in 1834 but the project bankrupted his firm and he turned to invention before returning to architectural practice and designing many distinguished, mainly Catholic churches. The church was dedicated to the Holy Name of Jesus but is known locally as 'Holy Name'. When completed between 1869–71 it was a massively prominent and ambitious church designed at a time when Catholics, at least in Lancashire, were no longer prepared to hide away in meagre buildings in back streets despite a general lack of money. The church is certainly large and it is moreover one of great architectural daring, more evident inside than out. Hansom favoured the thirteenth-century French Gothic style, using ideas inspired by the cathedrals at Amiens and Reims – hence the loftiness of the church, the sturdy west tower, the polygonal apse at the east end and a number of features inside. The west tower adjacent to the road was originally intended to have a spire half as

The broad but shallow chancel is surrounded by an apse passage and has an elaborate 'benedictional' altar.

The west end has an entrance vestibule below and a grand organ gallery above.

high again but the soft ground below would not allow it. An octagonal top added in 1928 is a perfect substitute. At the belfry stage the tower has a stone rood. The bells behind play a hymn tune on the hour from a repertoire of twenty. Most of the church behind the tower is hidden from the street because of adjacent university buildings. It is built of buff sandstone.

Inside, the church is almost as wide as it is long. The tall, very slender piers that support the wide-spanning arches and a rib-vaulted roof above are part of Hansom's architectural daring. It creates a sense of airiness reminiscent of the great late-medieval East Anglian parish churches. Hansom used cream-coloured terracotta rather than stone for the roof to reduce the structural load on the piers and, curiously, used it as a facing material throughout the interior. Its colour is not significantly different from the stone outside. The internal planning took into account some traditional requirements of a Jesuit church. The short length but great width of the church has the twofold purpose of

allowing all the congregation to be as close as possible to the altar and to see the prominent pulpit, for the Jesuits, a learned order, are noted for their preaching. (One recalls the similar requirements of eighteenth-century Anglicanism (pages 12, 54, 84) and of Methodism.) The high altar in a Catholic church was of course of central importance. In order that it should be as close as possible to the people the chancel is broad but shallow. Arches leading into the ambulatory that surrounds it are to be seen to the left and right of the altar. The latter is of the 'benedictional' type. This means that it has a tiered structure, with a canopied platform above the centre on which the gold or silver monstrance is placed to display the consecrated host at the service of benediction, usually an afternoon or evening service. At the opposite end of the church, the west end has an entrance vestibule and a huge organ gallery above. The north aisle has a row of no less than eight confessionals while the south has a series of chapels separated from it by terracotta screens with open tracery.

It is understandable that the church has many statues and pictures of Jesuit saints such as the founder St Ignatius Loyola and St Francis Xavier, who evangelised the Far East in the seventeenth century. Unlike most Catholic churches the interior has not been significantly re-ordered in the wake of the Second Vatican Council of the 1960s. A benedictional high altar at which the priest necessarily had his back to the people at mass is now a rarity in England, being substituted in new churches, or replaced in older churches, by a plain wooden table at which the priest faces the congregation. (In some Victorian churches splendid older marble structures have been retained, the newer tables merely inserted in front, a happy compromise.) Late-nineteenth-century Catholic devotional attitudes made strong appeals to the emotions, evident in the church statues, shrines and pictures of the time. Although they too have been reduced in most churches they are much in evidence in Holy Name. Diversity in such matters is surely to be welcomed to suit different preferences.

When the Jesuits commissioned Hansom to build their church in Oxford Road in 1869 they were probably only little aware that a small institution of higher education called Owens College founded in the city in 1851 was rapidly expanding. In 1870 it was purely coincidental that its governing body commissioned the leading architect of public buildings in the late nineteenth century, Alfred Waterhouse, to design and site their first major buildings just fifty yards away from the church on the opposite side of the road. They are arranged around a quadrangle in massive Victorian Gothic style. 'Owens' as it was then commonly known became the first constituent college of the Victoria University in 1880, later being joined by similar colleges in Liverpool and Leeds. Owens gained its charter as the independent University of Manchester in 1904. It was in the vanguard of the 'redbrick' universities (a term coined much later, and Waterhouse's buildings are of stone, not red brick). The university grew only relatively slowly until the 1960s when it shared in the explosion of higher education that has continued ever since. The grand church that the Jesuits built in 1869 is now surrounded by equally grand university

The nave arcade is made up of slender piers supporting a rib-vaulted roof.

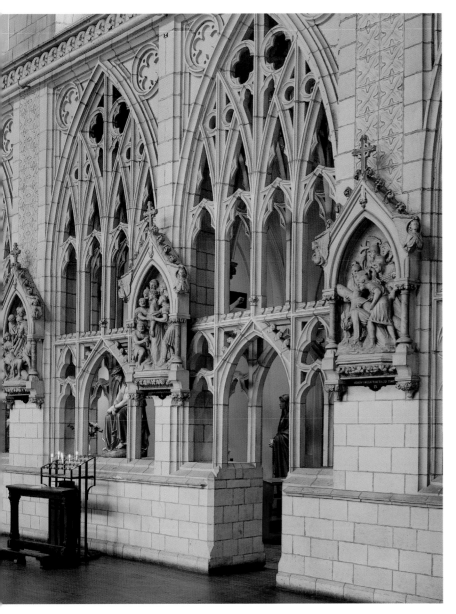

The south aisle screen of terracotta leads into a series of side-chapels.

The statue of St Francis Xavier, a seventeenth-century Jesuit saint who worked in the Far East, is one of many reminders that the church was founded by the order.

buildings. Its nearest neighbours are the Medical School to one side and the Students' Union building on the opposite side of the street. The University of Manchester Institute of Science and Technology (UMIST) now formally united with the Victoria University, the Manchester Metropolitan University (formerly Manchester Polytechnic) and the Royal Northern College of Music are all adjacent, making Oxford Road the largest urban education precinct in Europe, where lecture halls, laboratories, administration buildings and students' halls of residence all intermingle. In term time, therefore, Holy Name sees thousands of students each day hurrying to lectures or dawdling with friends. These photographs were taken in a week in mid-July when for several days in brilliant sunshine thousands of students gowned and hooded in a great variety of colours depending on their faculty were joined by proud families at an endless succession of graduation ceremonies.

ACCESS

The church is always open every day from 7 a.m. until dusk. There are at least two services each day.

ST PHILIP, SALFORD, GREATER MANCHESTER

A COMMISSIONERS' CHURCH FOR A GROWING GEORGIAN TOWN

The centre of eighteenth-century Salford was on the banks of the River Irwell, where it makes a series of serpentine loops less than a mile from Manchester city centre and its cathedral (page 78). Only traces of this older Salford survive in the form of little clusters of elegant terraced houses, and the oldest of its churches, Sacred Trinity. Modern day Salford, although vastly bigger, has acquired no other clearly defined centre; the docks and various business and shopping areas are scattered around widely. So if Salford today has a centre it is still at the same place as two or three hundred years ago, showing how the cities of Salford and Manchester have developed so uniquely close to one another.

St Philip's church was built in 1822–4 to serve this riverside Georgian community. It was strategically sited in a small square about thirty yards off the busy Chapel Street (known to motorists today as the A6) leading from Manchester to Chorley. A narrow cobbled street linked the square to this main road so that from the latter the fine church portico was visible to passing pedestrians or riders. Only a little of the square and it adjacent streets have survived later nineteenth- and twentieth-century encroachment but it still remains a quiet hidden little enclave, close as it is to the incessant traffic on the A6. The architect of St Philip's was Sir Robert Smirke (1780–1867). Smirke was one of the leaders of the 'Greek Revival' movement in early-nineteenth-century English architecture, which looked back to ancient Greece for its models rather than to the later Roman Empire or the fifteenth-century Italian Renaissance. Smirke is perhaps best known as the architect of the British Museum in London (1823–46). St Philip's was a 'Commissioners' Church'. In 1818 Parliament voted £1 million for new churches and a further half million in 1824. The drift of people from the country to cities led to the growth of urban parishes so that some then exceeded 500,000 people. The clergy persuaded the government that parishes required sub-division with provision of new churches. Also the English Establishment at this time had been greatly alarmed by the success of the French Revolution and was afraid that the atheism, anti-monarchial and anti-capitalist sentiments and violence associated with them might spread to England. The continuing moderating influence of the national church was regarded as a bastion against such things reaching this side of the Channel. Church Building Commissioners were appointed to administer the funds and it is these who gave their name to the new churches. In the event some 600 churches were built under the Act between 1818–56 when the fund was wound up. The churches are also sometimes known as 'Waterloo Churches' in the mistaken belief that Parliament voted the money to celebrate the victory in the battle of 1815. A number of guidelines were laid down by the Commissioners. The churches were to be 'economically' built without excessive ornament, a limit of £20,000 being set for any one church (St Philip's cost £14,670). Seating was to be provided for 1,000–2,000 people and at least half of these seats were to be

ABOVE RIGHT The main portico of the church in a little square faces down to one of Salford's principal thoroughfares nearby.

RIGHT The three-sided gallery dominates the interior. It was designed to provide 'economical' seating for over 1,000 people.

free for the poor. (High pew rents were common previous to this and remained so in other churches.) All seats were to have a view of the pulpit and were to be within earshot of the preacher. However, the pulpit was not to be so large or so placed as to obstruct a view of the altar as was sometimes the case in Non-Conformist churches and some Anglican churches belonging to its Puritan wing. No particular architectural style was laid down: architects might use Gothic or Classical according to their skills and the preferences of their clients. Despite the emphasis on 'economy', several of the most distinguished architects of the day were employed for Commissioners' churches to create many good buildings.

Because of Smirke's strong preferences, St Philip's was a classical church and conformed to the conditions laid upon him. The church has a rectangular ground plan with slightly projecting corners. The most prominent feature externally (which must have taken up a high proportion of Smirke's allowance) is the grand portico and tower above. The portico has slender Ionic columns supporting a parapet. Above that the round tower has diminishing stages terminating in a domed cap. The original clock survives near the top. This area of Salford has as yet few tall modern buildings so the tower is visible from considerable distances. The windows are in two tiers: small square ones below, tall round-headed ones above, the reason for this being apparent inside.

The interior is impressive because of the galleries around three sides. Only in this way could the Commissioners' required seating numbers be met. The galleries are supported from below by short piers of rectangular section but most strikingly they themselves support the roof by tall Greek Doric columns, much slimmer than those of antiquity from which they supposedly derive. The galleries are lit by the tall round-headed windows and the lower space below by the square ones.

There is a white marble monument to Brevet Major Charles Shaw, killed in 1842 'during the Afghanistan campaign'. His plumed hat, sword and rifle are carved above the inscription. To a visitor today the monument brings past and recent British military history together in a particularly vivid way as since 2001 British soldiers have fought for the Afghanistan government against Taliban insurgents and more than a hundred have followed Charles Shaw to their deaths there.

Thirty years ago, on my first visit to St Philip's, its immediate surroundings were in a depressing state. Most of the Georgian square had, as described, vanished long before that, never to be re-instated, but it was the legacy of later nineteenth- and twentieth-century industrial and domestic building and subsequent dereliction that was appalling. Happily things have improved considerably and will probably continue to do so as part of the general urban regeneration of the north in the last ten years. One of the streets leading off the square has a short row of eighteenth-century terraced houses, which includes the vicarage, and these are all in excellent condition. The fact

that the side of the (former) Royal Salford Hospital abuts the square does the church no favours, nor does one small scruffy business premises. However, the church has a railed off area of ground a few yards wide on three sides, within which a line of trees marches with military precision parallel to the church, nicely matching its rectangularity. To the east, slum property has been cleared and grassed over. From fifty yards or so beyond this the council has built many attractive modern houses (not a high rise block in sight) in well-laid-out streets with an almost rural abundance of small trees in gardens and on pavements, giving a positively leafy atmosphere in summer. Urban councils and their planners have learnt the lessons from the disasters of the 1950s and 1960s. Given a few more years the former Georgian residents of the little square might find this a pleasant place to return to.

ACCESS

It is not generally possible to leave the church open.

ABOVE The church was built in 1822–4 by Sir Robert Smirke, architect of the British Museum in London. The prominent tower is visible over much of the area.

LEFT This monument to a soldier killed in Afghanistan in 1842 has a resonance in modern times as many British soldiers have died in that country fighting Taliban insurgents.

ST HELEN, SEFTON, MERSEYSIDE

A LATE-MEDIEVAL CHURCH WITH FINE FURNISHINGS HERALDING THE RENAISSANCE

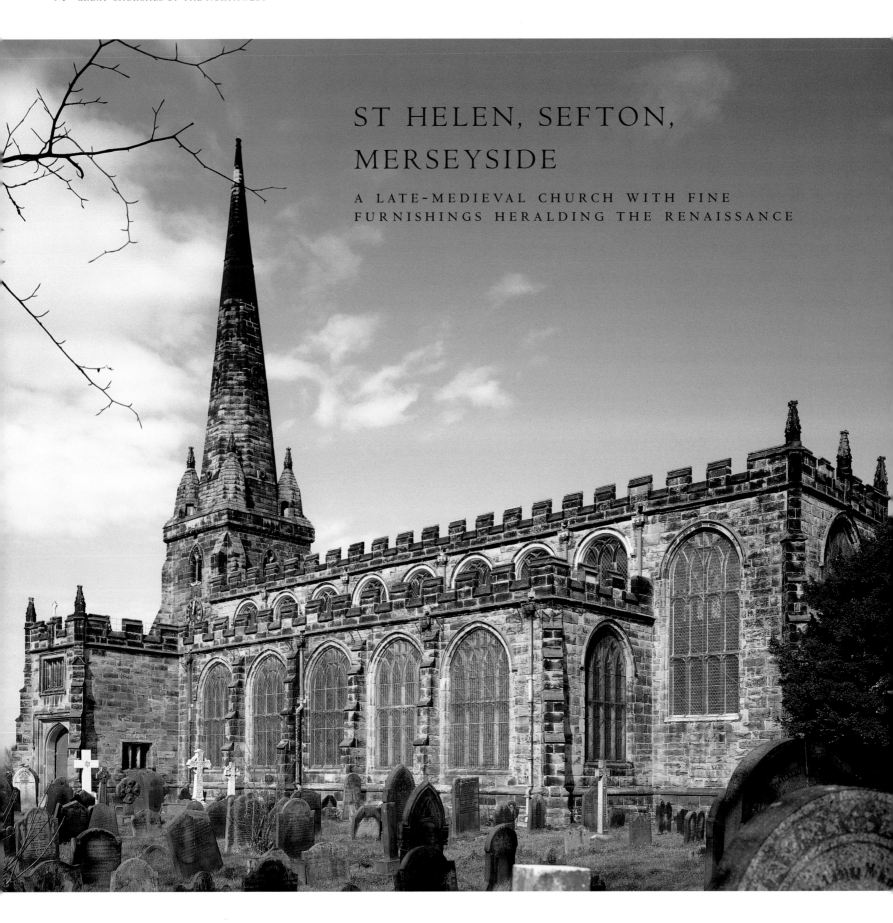

Sefton village is about eight miles northeast of Liverpool city centre, in the flat landscape of the Lancashire coastal plain. For a hundred years or more the suburbs of the city have crept ever closer and today the village maintains its separate identity by a ring of countryside only a few fields wide. Hopefully planning restrictions will keep that barrier intact, free from further 'development'. More recently the village has given its name to a new metropolitan borough of which it is at the approximate centre. The church has an old pub next door and about thirty houses clustered around it. A medieval hall, the home of the Molyneux family (see below), a sixteenth-century mill and a Georgian rectory have all gone. In the Middle Ages the parish extended many miles beyond the village on all sides, typical of the large parishes of northern England (see Preface). The church spire is a prominent feature at great distances in this type of landscape, just like a Lincolnshire fenland church.

From the churchyard the exterior south side is a textbook example of an entirely and uniformly Perpendicular Gothic church. One is immediately struck by the way in which, characteristically, the aisle wall is more glass than stone. The window tracery has that network of mullions closely ascending into the tops of the arches that gives the style its name. Despite this Perpendicular uniformity on the south side, traces of an earlier church survive. The northeast chapel has Decorated Gothic windows and inside there is on display a 'waterleaf' capital characteristic of the decade 1190–1200. The stone, although buff coloured, belongs to the New Red Sandstone of south Lancashire. The Perpendicular rebuilding of the church was carried out between 1490–1550, a turbulent period that saw the first, Henrician, stage of the Reformation acted out in England. The work was sponsored by three successive rectors, all members of the Molyneux family. The head of the family was the hereditary patron of the living who followed the not unusual tradition in England of presenting younger sons as rectors.

The interior of the church is typically Perpendicular too. Its slim arcade piers have the characteristic four subsidiary shafts separated by deep hollows. The later Middle Ages liked spatially simple, clear interiors exemplified here by the lack of any architectural division between the nave and chancel. The church is famous for its 'marvellous wealth of fitments, especially the gorgeous display of screens'

LEFT The south side of the church is more glass than stone, which is typical of Perpendicular Gothic architecture, in this case 1490–1550.

RIGHT The early-sixteenth-century chancel screen is one of seven screens in the church, all sumptuously carved.

The upper part of the chancel screen has a ribbed coving with cresting above.

The dado of the screen has putti holding shields, a remarkably early example of Renaissance motifs. The initial I stands for J[ames] Molyneux, rector at the time.

(Pevsner). They are all contemporary with the rebuilding and they can hold their own with anything in East Anglia and Lincolnshire. The woodwork was sensitively restored in 1907–22 by W.D. Caröe, one of the most distinguished architects of the early twentieth century. He lived locally and sang in the choir as a boy. Those parts of the roof, screens or pews that had deteriorated beyond the point of conservation were replaced in a way that almost defies detection The major piece of work is the richly carved chancel screen. It has a ribbed coving with cresting above. The dado (lower part) has shields held by putti, a remarkably early example of Renaissance motifs anywhere in England for this date, especially so in the north. There are six more screens in the church: between the chancel and side chapels, between the chapels and the aisles, and a screen around the Sefton (Molyneux) pew. The chancel has a complete set of early-sixteenth-century choir stalls. The benches have carved ends and poppy heads (page 11). The pulpit is a century later, dated 1635; its backplate and sounding board are preserved. The classical altar reredos was given by Anne Molyneux in 1730. There are a number of monuments and funeral hatchments to two (unrelated) Blundell families, local landowners who lived in two large mansions at Little Crosby and Ince Blundell near by. The fact that both these families were staunch Catholic recusants shows that, despite antagonistic religious attitudes nationally, there were close and warm relationships locally here. (In fact Nicholas Blundell of Little Crosby, a noted diarist in the early eighteenth century, was actually a churchwarden at Sefton – while paying monthly fines for his non-attendance at this, his parish church.)

The Molyneux family who built the original church in the late twelfth century, rebuilt it in the sixteenth and provided several rectors, moved to Croxteth on the east side of Liverpool in the eighteenth century, built a mansion there and were created Earls of Sefton. Since then they have been prominent in Liverpool public life (page 110). They have little connection with the church now but a modern plaque commemorates their contributions to it.

Had Sefton been closer to Liverpool much of all the things described above would doubtless have been swept away in a Victorian restoration. In this respect the remoter churches were the lucky ones.

ACCESS
It is not possible to leave the church open but it welcomes visitors on bank holidays and heritage weekends in summer.

OPPOSITE
ABOVE LEFT The Jacobean pulpit dated 1635 has the most intricately carved surfaces

ABOVE RIGHT The chancel reredos dates from 1730, a striking classical insertion into a Gothic church.

BELOW LEFT An eighteenth-century funeral hatchment of Nicholas Blundell, a prominent local Catholic recusant and diarist.

BELOW RIGHT A modern plaque commemorating the contributions of the Molyneux family, now Earls of Sefton, to the church over many centuries.

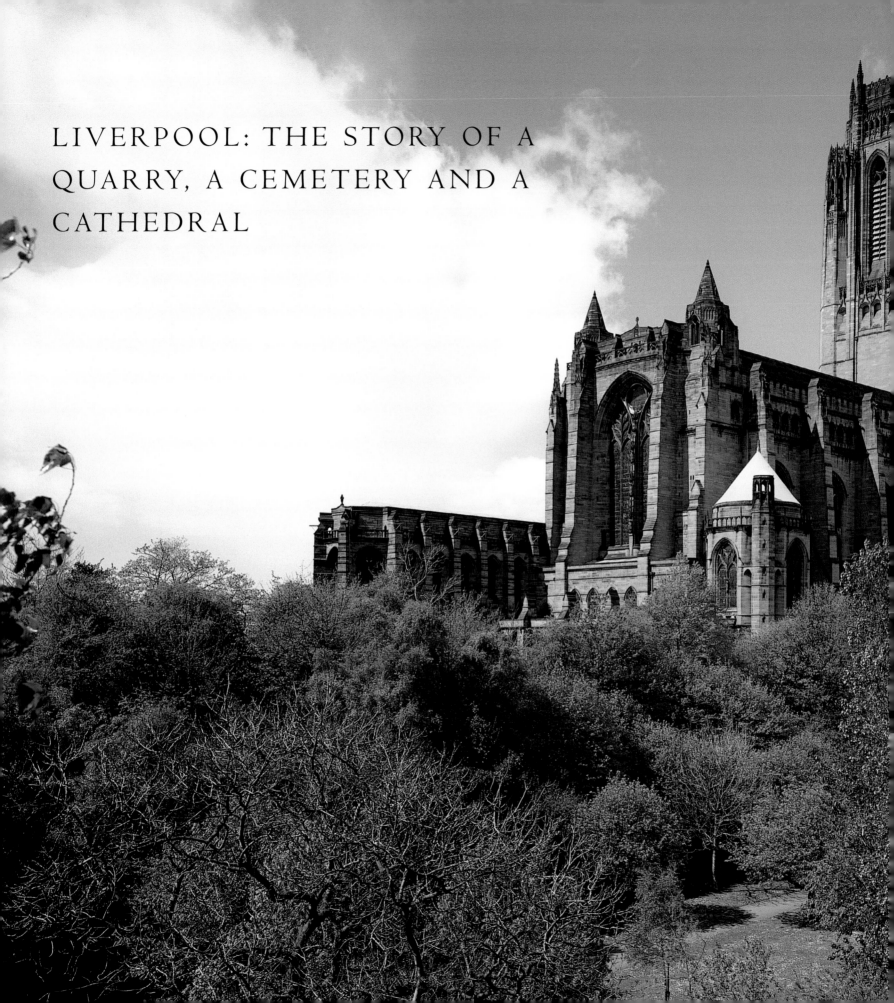

LIVERPOOL: THE STORY OF A
QUARRY, A CEMETERY AND A
CATHEDRAL

Liverpool became an Anglican diocese in 1880, thirty-three years after its arch-rival Manchester (pages 78–81). Spiritual needs apart, its creation was no doubt driven by the civic and commercial competition between the two cities which was just as intense then as between their football supporters today. Before that Liverpool, like Manchester, was part of the diocese of Chester. For the first twenty years a city-centre church served as a pro-cathedral but unlike Manchester it was decided to build a large purpose-designed cathedral on an ambitious scale (to outmatch Manchester by far) and so the choice of an appropriate site was important. To see what was available we must briefly go back a little in time.

At the end of the seventeenth century, Liverpool was starting to expand from the small medieval fishing port that it had been since the thirteenth century. The first cargo ship had already crossed the Atlantic to America and plans were envisaged for the first stone dock. The merchants and gentry who were profiting from increasing trade wished to move out of the crowded medieval streets bordering the River Mersey in the area known affectionately to Liverpudlians now as the Pier Head. Inland from the river the land remains flat for

LEFT In the foreground is the stone quarry converted into 'the most romantic cemetery in England'. The cathedral was later imaginatively sited along its edge overlooking the city.

BELOW The quarry rockfaces were used to excavate vaults for burials of the rich, cut into the sandstone rock. Above at street level there is a glimpse of Georgian Liverpool.

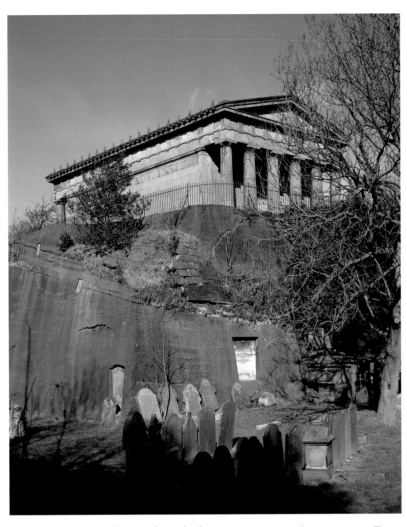

Perched on the edge of the rockface of a former quarry converted to a cemetery, The Oratory, built in 1827 as the cemetery chapel, is an exquisite replica of a Greek Doric temple. The entrance front of the cathedral is immediately to the left on the upper level.

In the centre of the cemetery is the mausoleum of William Huskisson, Liberal MP for Liverpool, killed at the opening of the Liverpool–Manchester railway in 1830. The later cathedral towers above it.

about half a mile and starts to rise quite steeply to a ridge that runs parallel to the river about a mile distant. At the beginning of the eighteenth century this was an ideal place for the wealthy to build new houses. In addition to brick, a source of stone was required for the many new civic buildings, churches and houses of a grander sort for the particularly wealthy. The ridge above the river looking down on the old town and its new docks is composed entirely of New Red Sandstone of a quality to provide good building stone. A quarry was opened and throughout the whole of the eighteenth century it provided a buff coloured stone for the expanding town. In the second half of the century and the first half of the nineteenth a local architect John Foster and his son, also John, designed a large part of Georgian Liverpool in the area adjacent to the quarry. It was a typical Georgian layout made up of a network of streets and small squares lined with large three- and four-storey terraced houses whose dignity and elegance derives from that simple symmetry of plan

and elevation and restrained decoration of which the Georgians were masters. The squares were provided with enclosed lawns and gardens at their centres in the manner of contemporary London squares. At the beginning of the nineteenth century the quarry was about 400 yards long, 100 yards wide and 50 yards deep with near vertical sides. By 1820 it was no longer considered economical to work further below this depth and the city corporation made the decision – the quite remarkable and, as it later transpired, brilliant decision – to lay out the disused quarry as a cemetery. John Foster Junior was commissioned and the necessary work was carried out in 1825–9. At the four corners of the quarry-cemetery he built four long ramps to take the horse-drawn hearses and carriages down to the graves and mausoleums. On one of the longer sides of the quarry he designed terraces to give access to the mausoleums planned to be cut out of the rock face as burial places for the wealthier families.

The cathedral seen from the Brunswick dock alongside the River Mersey. On a high ridge it dominates the city centre and the riverside as its planners intended. The Brunswick dock formerly used for timber imports is now a yachting marina.

The result was called St James's Cemetery after St James's church about 200 yards away, a simple classical brick building of 1775. However, the cemetery was provided with its own mortuary chapel, sometimes known as The Oratory, also designed by John Foster Junior. He chose a site at the northwest corner of the cemetery right at the edge of the precipitous drop to the former quarry floor below. Foster was a distinguished classical architect who had not only travelled in Greece but had carried out archaeological excavations there. (It was the period of European architectural history known as the Greek Revival when Greek models were preferred to Roman.) His chapel is an accurate and exquisite miniature replica of a Greek Doric temple, perfect in its detail. The 'temple' has six columns at each end, one of which faces the river and the other the quarry. Pevsner described it as 'a noble exterior and a noble interior'. When seen from among the graves in the quarry below it appears as what must surely be the most dramatically

sited chapel in England. It soon became filled with fine neo-classical monuments in white marble to Liverpool worthies of the time.

The planting of trees in the centre of the quarry and the growth of ivy and other creepers over its stone faces have with time removed the starkness that the original must have had so that today it has been described 'as the most romantic cemetery in England'. For a hundred years the great and the humble of Liverpool were buried here. The most prominent monument is the mausoleum of William Huskisson, the Liberal M.P. for the city who was killed when he fell beneath the wheels of the steam engine at the opening of the Liverpool–Manchester passenger railway, the first in the world, opened on 15 October 1830. The monument too was designed by Foster Junior, a handsome domed circular temple again based on a Greek model. The statue of Huskisson, which until recently could be viewed through a grille-door, is now in a city museum. Elsewhere in the cemetery is a line of gravestones for

people at the other end of the social scale; each records the names and ages of up to twenty children who died of typhoid in city orphanages in the late nineteenth century. Near by is the grave of the legendary Kitty Wilkinson, who, although of the poorest herself, campaigned successfully for the building of bathhouses and laundries in the city's slums.

In 1825 the city fathers had made the inspired decision to convert the disused quarry into a cemetery. In 1901 the Anglican Church authorities made the equally inspired decision to build their planned cathedral on the longer edge of the cemetery, which would create a massive new neighbour for Foster's mausoleum chapel. From here on the ridge overlooking the River Mersey it would in time, they foresaw, come to dominate the city centre and the docks, which indeed it has. Likewise the view of the cathedral from the quarry below would be no less dramatic. The competition held to select a design attracted entries from one hundred and three architects. The one chosen was from Giles Gilbert Scott, a young man only twenty-two years old but whose pedigree was impeccable: his family had dominated English church architecture throughout the second half of the nineteenth century. Gothic had, as we have seen, been the favoured style throughout this period and Scott like most of the competitors submitted Gothic drawings. His cathedral has been described as 'the final flowering of the Gothic Revival as a vital creative movement and is one of the great buildings of the twentieth century'. Most of the funding came from Liverpool's merchant class anxious to have their city's greatness proclaimed to the world at large, and no doubt to Manchester in particular. It was entirely appropriate that the stone also came from Liverpool, New Red Sandstone from the Woolton area of the city – and it really is red here. This stone was used for the entire building, at least in all parts that are visible and the traditional cutting and carving methods were used. Building was started in 1904 but because of its size, the slow traditional methods of construction and the intervention of two world wars it was not finally completed until 1978, although much of the cathedral was operational long before that.

Scott's design, said to be the largest cathedral in England, is a personal and distinguished use of the Gothic idiom, in no way an attempt to copy its medieval predecessors. Seen from any viewpoint the immediate overall impression is one of massive and very solid bulk. Although there are decorative elements, such as traceried parapets, pinnacles, turrets, finials and the like, they have to be looked for and they count for little from the middle distance in contrast to, say, the medieval cathedrals at Gloucester or Lincoln. This seems entirely appropriate in a northern city setting. When seen from a more considerable distance the eye identifies simply two intersecting solid blocks: the horizontal (nave and chancel) and the vertical (the great central

The nave seen from the chancel is a single gigantic room crossed by a bridge at its west end.

tower). There are two sets of transepts both quite close to the centre of the building and it is a curious feature of the design that the space between is occupied on both sides by broad flights of steps leading to two equally wide porches. Functionally these serve little purpose because the main entrances for both everyday and ceremonial use are at the west end of the cathedral. The steps and porch on the north side seem particularly redundant because they lead out only onto the edge of the quarry. The Lady Chapel at the east end is parallel to the chancel and not a continuation of it as in most major medieval churches. It is connected to the chancel by a short two-sided link and is as large as an average parish church.

The greater part of the interior is one large open space made up of an aisleless nave in which the absence of dividing piers draws the eye to the walls and once again, as outside, this creates a sensation of solidity. The two pairs of transepts already referred to have a considerable projection but play little part in either the functional use of the cathedral or the aesthetic effect. There is a curious feature internally as there is outside. On entering through the west door visitors find themselves in what appears as a large vestibule to the nave. It is the height and width of the building but as the nave beyond is reached only by a flight of steps the main body of the church is almost invisible from this area. It is separated from the nave by a bridge-gallery, a most distinctive feature. At the other end of the nave the tall, wide chancel is lit by a large east window and by smaller side windows but because the former is filled with very dark stained glass and the latter are high up the effect is rather dark; the gilded reredos has to be continuously illuminated to be seen. The bishop's stone throne or 'cathedra' (which gives the building its name) is an impressive structure. Throughout the cathedral there is much attractive stained glass in rich colours. The Lady Chapel is so separate from the main body of the church that it has to be sought out. It is one of the most attractive parts of the cathedral where services for smaller congregations can be held. The tall and massive central tower can be ascended by visitors, partly by lift, partly by stairs. From the roof there are magnificent views across the city, the docks and the river.

This great church is undoubtedly the swan song of a particular age of architecture. Nothing like this will ever be built in England again. The scale, the design, the materials and methods of construction, the financial investment and perhaps also the necessary will all belong to another age. Giles Gilbert Scott spent the whole of his professional life actively engaged in the ongoing design of his cathedral and the problems that it posed – ongoing because Scott changed his plans as building proceeded almost as frequently as Sir Christopher Wren changed his plans during the building of St Paul's Cathedral. Scott died in 1961 without seeing the cathedral quite finished and although a Catholic (a fact that caused some consternation in 1901) he is buried beneath a small plaque on the ground in front of the main entrance. The very unrepeatability of this cathedral is what makes it so important. What can be built and what has been built today can be seen half a mile away at the very contrasting Catholic cathedral (page 116), which by comparison some see as more ephemeral and transient. Scott's building seems as solid and enduring as anything that man can create and it will certainly outlast much of what is around it.

And what is around it? In all these portraits the importance and the effects of a church's surroundings have been noted. In the late 1970s, when the last stone at the west end of the cathedral was put in place, the surroundings of the great building were not an attractive sight. St James's Cemetery and St James's church itself were abandoned and derelict. In the adjacent streets and squares the Georgian houses were mainly divided into flats and much neglected and run down. The city below the cathedral had changed little since Victorian and Edwardian times except that its fine public buildings and almost everything else were covered in more soot and grime than ever before. More unhappily the people had lost some of their morale as many of the docks had closed, designed as they were for ships and working methods of several generations ago. Employment in other areas was also in drastic recession, not helped by poor industrial relations. For a short period Toxteth, the area adjacent to the cathedral was engulfed in riots. The city council was in political turmoil and financial crisis as arguments raged as to what should be done.

After 1980 something was done. St James's Cemetery was designated as St James's Gardens and is now attractively maintained by the council. The majority of visitors to the cathedral probably never go down the ramp between The Oratory and the cathedral to explore this area, thereby missing not only the exciting sight of the cathedral towering far above but also a glimpse of some of the eighteenth- and nineteenth-century history of the city. St James's church nearby should also be visited. It is no longer needed for worship and has been placed in the care of the Churches Conservation Trust (pages 32, 51), which will guarantee its future as the Trust proceeds slowly with restoration. Landlords of the Georgian property in the surrounding streets are restoring them to their former elegance. The area immediately below the cathedral, which had been a slum in the 1960s, has now attractive new housing in landscaped grounds. A little further afield down the hill in the city centre and alongside the river the skyline is at the time of writing pierced by the gantries of giant cranes as the shopping area and the river front are being transformed by new buildings of every kind in an unmistakably modern idiom creating a contrast with the more solid looking Victorian commercial premises. All this, of course, is very much a catching up with Manchester (page 85), which started its own resurgence ten

years ago and it is part of the same age-old rivalry referred to earlier. Fifty years ago it was said that the city was getting an Anglican cathedral worthy of it. Now it might be said that the cathedral was getting a city that was worthy of *it*.

ACCESS

The cathedral is open every day. There is adequate car parking within its own grounds. There is a visitor centre, shop and two cafés. St James's Gardens (quarry-cemetery) is open every day. The Oratory is open only rarely, administered by Liverpool Museums Service.

The bishop's throne or 'cathedra' which gives the building its name. Like the cathedral itself it is cut from local red sandstone.

ST JOHN THE BAPTIST, TUEBROOK, LIVERPOOL

A COLOURFUL INTERIOR WITHIN A MODEST EXTERIOR

The building of a new church today is generally initiated on a central diocesan basis involving the bishop and various advisory committees and then carried through by a diocesan architect subject to well-defined financial limits. Many of the most memorable churches of the Victorian period were, however, the product of a partnership between a wealthy private patron and a leading architect who between them went to extraordinary expense and extraordinary efforts to create an interior of sublime beauty that in the words of John Betjeman 'would bring people to their knees'. These private patrons might typically be an Earl, a landed baronet, a clergyman (often building his own parish church), a successful business man or an elderly spinster. We would expect such patrons to be Christians of some conviction and piety but it should be appreciated that the architects they commissioned generally shared their beliefs and piety. Among them were men such as A.W.N. Pugin and his son; George Gilbert Scott, his sons and grandsons; William Butterfield; G.F. Bodley; G.E. Street and J.L. Pearson. Some of the great Victorian architects lived and worked into the Edwardian period and even, in the case of Sir Ninian Comper into the latter half of the twentieth century. Although in their church building they worked as professionals, the spirit of their beliefs infused that work. Several were High Churchmen (Tractarians in the ecclesiastical language of the time) who worked best in

Completed in 1870 this Gothic Revival church has something of the quiet charm of a medieval village church, different from the bold assertiveness of many Victorian churches.

The Victorian love of surface decoration in all kinds of buildings is seen in this stencilling that covers the walls overall.

The upper part of the rood screen has coving and a loft parapet very much in the medieval tradition (see page 96).

designing churches for similarly minded patrons and clergy. The next two churches described in this book were the product of this type of Victorian piety, philanthropy and dedicated skills.

Tuebrook is a Liverpool suburb about three miles northeast of the city centre, mainly residential although the principal thoroughfare is an arterial road leading to and from an outer city ring road. It passes through a network of narrow streets lined with small but sturdily built Victorian and Edwardian houses. The church of St John the Baptist adjoins the road near to a particularly busy road junction. It is a church of modest size and unassuming exterior that does not immediately attract attention even from people who look at any church in a noticeing way. Yet this is a church produced by the type of partnership described above: Mrs J. Reade, the wife of a clergyman who gave £25,000 (about £2 million today) and George Frederick Bodley (1827–1907). In the 1840s Bodley worked in the office of George Gilbert Scott one of the first of the outstanding Victorian architects much influenced by Pugin (and the grandfather of Giles Gilbert Scott who was to be the architect of the city's Anglican cathedral, pages 98–104). Following Scott his first churches were in a bold, assertive, 'muscular' Gothic style based on French precedents. He later turned to the gentler more refined style of English Decorated Gothic of the thirteenth century. Tuebrook church, built 1868–70, reflects that in its unassuming plan, elevation and detailing. Most

prominent naturally is the steeple. It is a tower with a slim recessed spire linked by flying buttresses springing from four corner pinnacles, a feature familiar from the Decorated churches of the East Midlands. To the east of this is an aisled nave and lower chancel. The church is built of pink sandstone with banding of buff sandstone, reflecting the Victorian liking for polychromy but here again in a subdued way unlike some of Bodley's contemporaries. Bodley's gentle style of Gothic here is more like that of a typical thirteenth century village church, appropriate in a suburb among small domestic buildings where it does not have to compete with factories, mills and office blocks.

Seen from outside it is not apparent that this church is famous by national as opposed to merely regional standards. Nor is the interior architecture especially striking. It is an orthodox plan with nave, two aisles and a chancel with side-chapels. It is the resplendent decoration, ablaze with colour that makes this one of the most famous Victorian churches in England: what Betjeman describes as the 'beauty of holiness'. In some ways it reflects the Victorian taste for colour in any of their architecture: domestic (quite humble houses as well as grand), town halls, hotels, railway stations

In the chancel the organ and its casing are incorporated into the overall decorative scheme of the church.

The high altar (left) and a side-altar (right) are typical of those in any Roman Catholic church of the time.

and even factories. But the exquisite quality of the work in this context reflects the patron's and the architect's desire to make a House of God as sublimely beautiful as possible. The decoration of walls, ceilings and woodwork usually deteriorates more quickly than the building itself (as any householder knows) and by 1968 the interior of the church was in poor condition. To celebrate its centenary S.E. Dykes Bower (1903–94) one of the greatest church decorators of the twentieth century was commissioned to do a restoration. (He was, *inter alia*, Surveyor of the Fabric at Westminster Abbey from 1951–73; clearly the people of Tuebrook church are used to employing only the best.) The glowing colours must now be very close to the original effect. The dominant ones are green, red and gilt, an opulently rich combination. The walls have stencilling all over. If this now seems strange to us, and perhaps rather overdone, it should be remembered that medieval town and even village churches were usually decorated overall in this fashion. It was either removed in line with Protestant ideas or simply allowed to fade away to save expense at times when people were less enthusiastic about their parish churches. The roof with its tie-beams and collar-beams is similarly decorated all over.

The high altar and the side-altars are exactly as they would have been in a contemporary Roman Catholic church. The parish has always been High

Colour above as well as below: the highly decorated ceiling and tie-beams of the roof.

The pulpit resplendent in green, red and gilt.

Anglo-Catholic. On the completion of the building the then Bishop of Chester, in whose diocese Liverpool then was, refused to consecrate the church until certain 'popish' furnishings were removed. (St Agnes, Sefton Park, pages 110–15, met with similar objections a little later.) The exquisite rood screen is very much in the medieval tradition with its coving and loft parapet. It should be compared with that at Sefton church (page 96). The pulpit too fits into the overall scheme as does the organ and its casing on the south side of the chancel. Morris & Co. did some of the glass.

The large vicarage at the southeast corner of the church is also by Bodley. Many of the churches described in this book are today the result of an ongoing process of extensions, partial rebuilding and refurbishment according to the needs of the time. The interior of St John the Baptist, thanks to those who use it and care for it, still reflects in its entirety the values, tastes and artistry of the single generation that built it, one which had brought the art of church decoration to a high point. In that respect it is like Brougham church and Pilling church: an architectural time capsule, although in this case one which is very much alive.

ACCESS

It is not generally possible to leave the church open outside of service times.

ST AGNES, SEFTON PARK, LIVERPOOL

VICTORIAN MUNIFICENCE AND ARCHITECTURE ON A GRAND SCALE

The church from the southeast showing the polygonal apse at the east end,
a feature of French rather than English Gothic.

The Sefton Park area of Liverpool was created in 1867 as both a park and an affluent residential suburb about three miles southeast of the city centre when the council purchased over 200 acres of agricultural land from the Earl of Sefton to be laid out as an open space for the hundreds of thousands of people who lived in crowded slum conditions in the city centre. The idea was not to create a conventional municipal park writ large with mown lawns and tidy flowerbeds, but rather something on the lines of Hyde Park and Regents Park in London where people could walk freely, play or picnic. A competition to design and lay out the park was won by the unusual combination of a Frenchman, Edouard André, chief gardener to the city of Paris and a Liverpudlian, Lewis Hornblower. André had helped in the design of the Bois de Boulogne in Paris and Hornblower in the laying out of the smaller private Princes Park near by in Liverpool. The flat featureless land bought from the Earl was made to rise and fall a little; trees were planted singly and in small and large groups; existing streams were diverted to create a serpentine lake; the rest was areas of natural grassland crossed by curving pathways. A little architecture was incorporated into the scheme. There are a number of grand entrances with lodges at various points. Within the park itself the finest architecture is the Palm House, a magnificent iron and glass conservatory (now restored after years of dereliction). The cost of buying the land and converting it into a park in this way was offset by reserving land at the outer edges for sale as building plots for mansions and large villas which were themselves to be attractively integrated into the landscaping. From 1872 onwards this was the beginning of an area of grand houses, which then spread out from the park's boundary into spacious and leafy roads adjoining.

The growth of the new residential area led to the building of several churches when wealthy patrons came forward to create buildings appropriate to their surroundings. One of these who had acquired a new residence here was H. Douglas Horsfall, a successful stockbroker and a member of a High Church family whose members between them built no less than seven mainly Anglo-Catholic churches in various parts of the city. He purchased a site in Ullet Road on the edge of the park and in 1883 commissioned John Loughborough Pearson (1817–97) to design a church. Pearson was one of the most distinguished of the Gothic Revival architects of the late nineteenth century. At the time of this commission he was building the monumental St Augustine's church in Kilburn, London, and Truro Cathedral in Cornwall.

The church from the southwest, the smooth bright brick ablaze in the sunlight. It has the tall, narrow proportions characteristic of French Gothic.

The chancel is surrounded by an ambulatory passage with much ornate stone carving.

Looking from the Lady Chapel into the ambulatory and the chancel beyond.

Pearson favoured the earliest, thirteenth-century, style of Gothic, particularly the Gothic of Northern France, the region in which Gothic had been created. The French style was for tall, narrow, i.e. spatially concentrated churches. Early English Gothic, the style evolved from it on this side of the Channel was characterised by lower elevations and more spreading ground plans ('French soars, English spreads'). Pearson commonly combined elements of both in his designs. He had a unique ability to create ingenious and complex spatial effects in a church. These included the creation of receding vistas formed when one arcade of piers gave into another, which in turn opened into a transept, a chapel or an ambulatory. He realised more than any of his contemporaries that a stone rib-vaulted roof was literally and metaphorically the crowning glory of a Gothic church. It is an expensive feature to include in

a church but Pearson was fortunate to design only for the wealthiest of clients – Horsfall in this instance paying £28,000 (about £2.3 million today) for the completion of St Agnes. Pearson was an example of the type of Victorian architect who combined his professional skills with a devout Christian faith. When commissioned to design a church he would retire to a short religious retreat, praying and receiving the sacrament. The parallels between St Agnes and the other Liverpool church of St John the Baptist described in the last chapter are striking. They were built within twenty years of one another; both were paid for by wealthy private patrons at approximately the same enormous cost; both were built for Anglo-Catholic clergy and congregations who wanted furnishings and who celebrated liturgies deplored by evangelical bishops of the time. The two buildings themselves, however, are in marked contrast to one another. At Tuebrook the interior decoration takes precedence over the architecture. At Sefon Park it is the architecture that one remembers, externally and internally, the decoration is secondary.

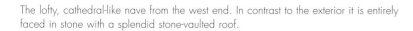

The lofty, cathedral-like nave from the west end. In contrast to the exterior it is entirely faced in stone with a splendid stone-vaulted roof.

The first impression of St Agnes externally is its size, particularly its height and its smooth, bright red brick. The effect of so much of this material is considerable and it is perhaps true to say that it is not so well regarded today as it was at the time it was built. Dark red sandstone is used for window and door dressings but hardly tells against the brighter brick. Its tallness contrasts with its narrowness in the French manner and another example of this is the polygonal apse at the east ending of the chancel. The English style would have been lower and broader and the chancel would have had a straight ending. English Gothic however is the projection of the two pairs of transepts near the east and west ends, a most unusual feature in a parish church. English too are the tall, narrow lancet windows used singly or in twos, threes or fours. There is no tower (the building could scarcely take any extra height), only a flèche over the crossing of the nave and eastern transepts. It is flanked by two turrets a little further east.

The first impression on entering the building is the strong, sweet smell of incense that is used regularly here and the relative dimness of the area where one is at first standing — a kind of lobby created by the gallery above. Typically of Pearson even this is vaulted and separated from the nave by an arcade. Beyond this in the nave is the first surprise: the interior is entirely faced with a buff-coloured stone in contrast to the brick outside. Surprising because most architects, today as then would choose to reverse this: stone outside, brick within. The nave roof has a splendid stone rib-vault, something that gives the church the noble character of a small cathedral. The nave is not long, just four bays,

The remarkable organ gallery creates a forest-like vista of columns when looking from the north-east transept into the chancel. It was an effect much-liked by the architect J.L. Pearson.

with a continuous triforium (wall passage) above the piers and a clerestorey above that. At the east end Pearson demonstrates his mastery of complex spatial effects in several places. The chancel has an ambulatory (a passageway with its own lower vaulted roof all around it) separated by a circle of piers with much rich carving above. To the south of the chancel is a Lady Chapel with an aisle alongside the ambulatory. On the other side of the chancel in the north transept is the organ which is integrated into the architecture by being mounted on an octagonal stone gallery supported by one central column and ten peripheral columns of black marble. This archetypal Pearson feature creates yet more vistas through a forest of columns towards the aisles and ambulatory. The furnishings are sumptuously in keeping with all this spatial grandeur. The alabaster pulpit carved with statues of Christ and the saints is supported by marble columns and the font is of the same materials. The altars and shrines around the church are exactly as they might be in a Roman Catholic church. Much of the rather dark glass is by C.E. Kempe, one of the most prolific of the late Victorian glaziers.

When the church was completed in 1884 Liverpool had only four years before become a diocese in its own right. Consequently the church was consecrated by the first bishop, John Charles Ryle, on 21 January 1885. As an echo of what had occurred at Tuebrook church in 1872 (pages 109), Ryle refused to induct the first vicar as planned on 24 March unless he gave an undertaking not to celebrate the Eucharist using certain Roman practices. The undertaking was given but it has not prevented the parish from maintaining a tradition of very high churchmanship. (In fact many of the 'ritualist' practices deplored by Evangelicals then are commonplace in all wings of the Anglican church today.)

Adjacent to the east end of the church is the red brick vicarage of 1885–7 by the noted domestic architect Norman Shaw.

Douglas Horsfall built three other churches in the Liverpool area. Even more significantly for the church nationally he founded what was to become St Chad's College in the University of Durham for the training of men for the Anglican ministry who could not afford to pay their own tuition fees. The college still holds the patronage of the living (the right to appoint the vicar) given to it by Horsfall.

Pevsner says of St Agnes church 'It is the noblest Victorian church in Liverpool', and there is no arguing with that.

ACCESS

It is not generally possible to leave the church open outside of services.

The font (top) and pulpit (below) are made of alabaster and marbles.

THE ROMAN CATHOLIC CATHEDRAL CHURCH OF CHRIST THE KING, LIVERPOOL

Roman Catholics account for about a fifth of the total population of Liverpool, a fraction higher than in any other English city. At the time of the Reformation Lancashire became a strongly recusant county where large numbers, including the aristocracy and gentry, refused to accept Henry VIII's claim to the title of head of the Church of England. In later centuries successive generations continued to be loyal to 'the Old Faith' despite harsh penal laws. In the mid-nineteenth century the number of native Catholics was greatly augmented by the immigration of people attempting to escape the Irish potato famine and that influx continued well into the twentieth century. Hence the very many Catholic churches in the city centre and the suburbs, large Victorian buildings often only a few hundred yards apart. Although the Catholic archdiocese was created in 1850 the city had no cathedral worthy of this large Catholic population. Since as early as 1853 plans had been in mind for a cathedral but nothing came of them as the authorities had other more pressing priorities and the overwhelmingly working class people were not in a position to provide the necessary finance. Until the 1960s a mean little church in a mean little back street behind the grand Adelphi Hotel served as a pro-cathedral.

In 1928, Richard Downey (1881–1953) was appointed as archbishop. He was an ambitious man, a genial but autocratic personality and an accomplished controversialist. He was aware that a uniquely high proportion of the city's population was Catholic and he also knew that the Catholics under his jurisdiction made up no less than half of all Catholics in England, far outnumbering for example those in the archdiocese of Westminster, the seat of the Cardinal-Archbishop, accepted leader of the English Catholic church. He must have had these facts vividly illustrated when in 1929, the year after his appointment, 400 thousand people attended a rally in the city to celebrate the centenary of the Catholic Emancipation Act that repealed many of the anti-Catholic penal laws. If architecture can in some way symbolise population then it was surely time for Liverpool to outmatch Westminster Cathedral, until then England's leading Catholic edifice. Downey would also have been very conscious that a great Anglican cathedral was slowly taking shape in the city centre (pages 98–104) and that too should be matched – or outmatched. He purchased a commanding site on the top of Mount Pleasant, part of the same ridge overlooking the River Mersey that the Anglican authorities had chosen for their cathedral a generation before and only half a mile away at the other end of Hope Street. In 1930 Downey commissioned Sir Edwin Lutyens (1869–1944), the leading architect of the day, to design a cathedral that would put the Catholic Cardinal and Archbishop of Westminster and the Anglican Bishop of Liverpool firmly in their places, together with their flocks. Lutyens designed a cathedral on a scale and grandeur never seen in England before and in few places elsewhere. It was a fusion of the eastern Byzantine style with Christopher Wren's style at St Paul's cathedral in London but with a feeling of modern austerity. A central dome was to be sixty feet higher than St Peter's in Rome, although perhaps in deference to papal sensitivities the cathedral as a whole was to be slightly smaller. The foundation stone was laid in 1933. By the outbreak of the Second World War, when work had to stop, even the crypt, vast as it was, had not been completed. Work resumed in a limited way in 1945 for about ten years as funds came in from a generous but by no means wealthy population. By the mid-1950s the cost of completing the cathedral had risen to about £400 million in today's values and the then archbishop decided that enough was enough. A plan to build a scaled down version by Adrian Gilbert Scott (brother of Giles Gilbert Scott, architect of the Anglican cathedral) was also abandoned. In 1959 a competition was held for a totally new design.

The approach and entrance front to the cathedral. It was built 1962–7 on a platform formed by the crypt of a previously planned but later abandoned cathedral. The circular plan and the large number of Liverpool-Irish Catholics have earned the cathedral the local nickname 'Paddy's Wigwam'.

An overall view of the circular interior with the high altar at the centre and side-chapels at the perimeter. Lighting is provided by vertical and horizontal strips of coloured glass and by the lantern above.

The conditions given to the competing architects were that it was to cost no more than £1 million (it eventually cost about five times that amount) and secondly that in accordance with modern liturgical thinking the whole congregation should be in close proximity to the priest celebrating mass at the high altar even when the cathedral was full. The competition was won from 300 applicants by Sir Frederick Gibberd (1904–84), an architect who as a young man was among the first in England to embrace the so-called International Modern Movement in architecture created in Germany in the 1920s.

Gibberd had the brilliant idea of using the plateau created by the roof of the huge existing crypt of Lutyen's cathedral as a podium on which to build his own. There was more than adequate space with room to spare for visitors to perambulate around and for open-air services and meetings. On the basis of the terms stipulated by the church authorities Gibberd's design was inevitably a 'central' plan, in which the high altar is at the middle of the cathedral with seating for the congregation arranged around it. This of course was very different from the 'longnitudinal' plan which Christians in the West had become accustomed to for over 1,500 years, in which the clergy officiated at one end, traditionally the eastern end, and the congregation stretched away to the west. It is quite wrong, however, to regard Gibberd's central plan as a wholly modern idea, as many people do. Christian architecture came into being when the emperor Constantine legalised Christianity in the Roman Empire in AD 313 and churches could be built openly for the first time. Christians were reluctant to use the pagan Roman temples as a model; instead they turned to the basilicas, buildings designed for general administrative and legal purposes which were found in every Roman city and town. They were aisled halls with a semi-circular extension (an apse) at one end for the use of a presiding official or magistrate. The latter was to become the highly developed chancel of a Christian church. The remaining rectangular part became the nave and aisles for the congregation and the building as a whole had a clearly longnitudinal form. (The fact that larger churches adopted a cruciform plan with transepts near the eastern end did not alter that.) Shortly after his legislation Constantine moved his seat as emperor away from Rome to Byzantium, renamed Constantinople, which had for long been the centre of the

RIGHT The central lantern is the largest stained glass window in the world. Designed by John Piper and Patrick Reyntiens it consists of three areas of colour: red (above), blue (centre) and amber-brown (below). Each is pierced by a splash of clear glass representing together the Holy Trinity.

BELOW More abstract glass in deep glowing colours in one of the side-chapels, also by Piper and Reyntiens.

eastern half of the empire. Rome remained the capital of the western half and the seat of the popes but as invasions of barbaric hordes from the north and the east increased Rome and the west declined rapidly throughout the fifth century and with it its art and architecture. In contrast the Byzantine Empire grew and flourished for nearly a thousand years. Unlike the west, church architecture was based on central plans from the start: circular, octagonal or Greek (equal-sided) crosses. The largest and most famous is Santa Sofia in Constantinople (now Istanbul), which is now a mosque. In the west central plans were adopted in a few places, notably Ravenna in northeast Italy, a meeting place of the eastern and western empires. It is worth noting too that in medieval England the Knights Templar always built circular churches in honour of the church of the Holy Sepulchre in Jerusalem founded by Constantine and near to which they had their headquarters. Later again, Italian architects of the Renaissance turned on several occasions to the central plan in the sixteenth and seventeenth centuries. Essentially, however, the whole of western Christendom, Catholic and Protestant retained the basilican plan right up to our own time. This apparent digression does enable us to understand that Gibberd and many other modern architects are simply returning to a very ancient plan, albeit quite strange to Christians in the west.

Gibberd's design is very simple. It is a circle 194 feet in diameter surrounded by side-chapels of widely varying plans and elevations. On the entrance side there is a prominently projecting entrance hall with a high open belfry above. From the top of the side walls a conical roof rises to a magnificent fully glazed tower (known as a lantern since it illuminates the interior) which in turn is surmounted by a circle of metal spikes. The whole structure is supported by prominent buttresses, which run down the conical roof and then from the top of the side walls they extend away from the walls to reach ground level in much the same way as guy ropes on a tent. Hence the cathedral's local nickname of 'Paddy's Wigwam'. Building took place from 1962–7. The materials used are white Portland stone from the Dorset coast and concrete. Only recently in 2004 has the originally planned grand approach to the entrance been completed in the form of a long, wide flight of steps rising from a piazza to the podium on which the cathedral is built, an arrangement somewhat reminiscent of St Paul's Cathedral in London

LEFT, ABOVE One of the many modern works of art gradually being installed in the cathedral: a striking metal statue of Abraham with the ram caught in the bush as described in the book of Genesis 22:13.

LEFT The chapel of the Holy Oils. The many side-chapels are used for a variety of purposes. Under the altar in this chapel are kept the oils blessed by the archbishop on Maundy Thursday and stored in three ampullae for use throughout the year in the sacraments of confirmation, ordination and the anointing of the sick.

RIGHT Varied geometry, light and shade: a view of two of the side-chapels and the sloping buttresses that surround the cathedral.

which is also built of Portland stone. At ground level there is a visitors' centre and restaurant with gardens above.

Because of the circular plan the interior reveals itself completely to visitors as soon as they enter. This is in contrast to the traditional basilican plan of medieval cathedrals, and the Anglican cathedral near by, whose long naves, aisles, transepts, chancel and side-chapels reveal themselves only gradually as one walks from west to east. Architecturally speaking this instant revelation of itself makes the building less interesting than others. Apart from the unusual plan what strikes first time visitors most is the cyclorama of colour that surrounds them in an interior that as a whole is quite dim even on a sunny day. Light is provided by a series of thin vertical strips of glass adjacent to the buttresses, which define the bays. These are joined up at the top by a horizontal strip of glass that runs all around the building. The colours are mainly deep blues and greens with some particularly vivid reds. Striking though this may be, many find it too garish, particularly the reds. To see the most spectacular stained glass in the cathedral one must move forward to the centre and look upwards into the lantern said to be the largest stained glass window in the world, about 12,500 square feet in area. The entirely abstract design is by John Piper, made by Patrick Reyntiens, two of the leading exponents of this art in the late twentieth century. There are three areas of colour, red, blue and brown-amber, each area having several shades merging into one another. In the centre of each there is a burst of clear light representing the Holy Trinity, Father, Son and Holy Spirit. The stained glass in the side chapels is mainly by these same two artists, also abstract using rich deep colours set in small geometric shapes.

It was stressed to the competing architects that the central high altar was the most important thing in the cathedral and that nothing must impede it or detract from it. It is cut from one large piece of white marble from Skopje in Yugoslavia. The whole of the circular chancel area is surmounted by a large bright metal baldacchino, designed by Gibberd, which hangs from the lantern.

As time goes by the cathedral is gradually acquiring a variety of furnishings and art works less abstract than those preferred by Gibberd as described above. Sean Rice has done a variety of work in metal, principally the fourteen Stations of the Cross with a silvered finish arranged around the walls. His also is a striking statue of Abraham with the ram he found caught in a bush as he was about to sacrifice his son at God's command. There are several tapestries, mosaics, carvings and paintings by other artists.

From the piazza at ground level or from the podium above outside the main door one sees down Hope Street to the Anglican cathedral, an orientation deliberately planned by Gibberd. The name of the street has in recent years be seen as symbolic from the point of view of Christian unity. At the time that the Lutyens crypt was started and the Anglican cathedral was half completed relations between Anglicans and Catholics were at best frosty and at worst antagonistic. But in the twenty-first century Liverpool Anglicans and Catholics pray and work together for Christian unity. In a broader context the whole city has a sense of hope too for the future.

ACCESS

The cathedral is open every day from early morning until evening. There is a visitors' centre, restaurant and bookshop.

RIGHT The view of the Anglican cathedral seen from the top of the steps in front of the Catholic cathedral. They are joined by Hope Street running down the centre of the picture. Its name has been seen as symbolic in terms of Christian unity.

EPILOGUE

It has happened fortuitously that the Bewcastle Cross on the Scottish border at the northern starting point of this journey and the Roman Catholic cathedral in Liverpool on the River Mersey at its southern finishing point are also the furthest apart in time, separated by about one hundred and fifty miles and thirteen hundred years. Again, no two places could be more different in their surroundings, one lonely and remote and the other at the heart of a great city. In the Preface it was said that the choice of churches on this journey through northwest England would be varied and comprehensive and the places we have visited bewteen Bewcastle and Liverpool have hopefully justified that claim. After Saxon Bewcastle church architecture of every century betwen the twelfth and the twentieth has been represented, on fells and moors, in villages, towns and cities. Like their counterparts in other parts of England the buildings represent a remarkable continuity of purpose and endeavour, expressing the same essential faith and ideals however much those may have varied in some outward forms over the centuries. It is a continuity that has few parallels elsewhere in the world.

The paradise window at St Martin, Brampton, shows angels holding musical instruments and scrolls welcoming the virtuous into heaven.

ACKNOWLEDGMENTS AND BIBLIOGRAPHY

The following have been used as sources of historical, architectural and technical data. They are all warmly recommended for further reading.

Nikolaus Pevsner: *The Buildings of England* (Penguin and Yale University Press). A monumental and unique series of architectural guides originally published 1951–74 in the form of forty-six county guides (some counties are covered by more than one volume). Each volume sets out to describe every building of any architectural merit or significance as personally inspected by Sir Nikolaus Pevsner (1901–83) a German emigré of prodigious erudition and energy. Most serious church explorers use the appropriate 'Pevsner' as an indispensable guide on their visits. They are now being extensively revised.

In the first editions of the series the area covered in this book was described in three volumes of the series:

Cumberland and Westmorland (Penguin, 1967)
Lancashire North (Penguin 1969)
Lancashire South (Penguin, 1969)

In the latest revised editions, *Lancashire South* has been republished in two greatly expanded volumes:

Lancashire: Liverpool and the Southwest (Yale University Press, 2006)
Lancashire: Manchester and the Southeast (Yale University Press, 2004)

John Betjeman: *Guide To English Parish Churches* (Collins, 1958, revised 1968). A selective guide to the more interesting churches in each county of England by an architectural writer and poet with an unrivalled and infectious 'passion for churches'.

Alec Clifton-Taylor: *The Pattern of English Building* (Faber & Faber, 1962). A very readable guide to traditional building materials, the geology, the quarries, the properties of the stones and the character of the buildings.

Alec Clifton-Taylor: *English Parish Churches as Works of Art* (Batsford, 1974). Every aspect of churches is covered: architectural styles, building materials and all their furnishings. An Appendix gives a list of the more outstanding churches in each county.

J.S. Curl (editor): *Oxford Dictionary of Architecture* (Oxford University Press, 1999). A good source for quick concise references for subjects from Perpendicular to piscina, Romanesque to rood screen as well as short biographies of architects, etc.

The Churches Conservation Trust. An organisation which cares for over 300 churches that are now no longer needed for public worship ('redundant' churches). The churches are often in remote country places but can be found in towns and cities. These churches are often wonderfully 'atmospheric' having escaped Victorian restorations because of their isolation and poverty. The Trust makes a point of providing maximum possible access to visitors and providing informative and welcoming literature. The Trust publishes free booklets giving information about its churches in each English county. Return postage costs are appreciated. The Churches Conservation Trust, 1 West Smithfield, London EC1A 9EE.